NEW ACCENTS

General Editor: TERENCE HAWKES

Superstructuralism

IN THE SAME SERIES:

*Not available from Methuen, Inc. in the USA

Superstructuralism

The Philosophy of Structuralism
and Post-Structuralism

RICHARD HARLAND

METHUEN

London and New York

First published in 1987 by
Methuen & Co. Ltd
11 New Fetter Lane, London EC4P 4EE
Reprinted 1988

Published in the USA by
Methuen & Co.
in association with Methuen, Inc.
29 West 35th Street, New York NY 10001

Photoset by Rowland Phototypesetting Ltd
Bury St Edmunds, Suffolk
Printed in Great Britain by
Richard Clay Ltd, Bungay, Suffolk

British Library Cataloguing in Publication Data

Harland, Richard
Superstructuralism: the philosophy
of structuralism and post-structuralism.
– (New accents)
1. Structuralism
I. Title   II. Series
149'.96   B841.4

ISBN 0-416-93232-X
ISBN 0-416-03242-7 Pbk

Library of Congress Cataloging in Publication Data

Harland, Richard, 1947–
Superstructuralism: the philosophy
of structuralism and post-structuralism.
(New accents)
Bibliography: p.
Includes index.
1. Structuralism – History.
I. Title.   II. Series:
New accents (Methuen & Co.)
B841.4.H37 1987   149'.96   86-23627

ISBN 0-416-03232-X
ISBN 0-416-03242-7 (pbk.)

When a man howls or shouts or threatens, we other animals understand him very well! Then his attention is not in that other world! But he barks in a way all his own – he speaks. And this has enabled him to invent what does not exist and to overlook what exists. As soon as he gives a thing a name he ceases to see the thing itself; he only hears the name that he gave it or sees it written. . . . For him, everything in the world is merely a pretext for talking to other men or for talking to himself.

Funeral oration, by Orfeo the dog on
Augusto the man, in Miguel de Unamuno's novel *Mist*

Contents

General editor's preface

It is easy to see that we are living in a time of rapid and radical social change. It is much less easy to grasp the fact that such change will inevitably affect the nature of those disciplines that both reflect our society and help to shape it.

Yet this is nowhere more apparent than in the central field of what may, in general terms, be called literary studies. Here, among large numbers of students at all levels of education, the erosion of the assumptions and presuppositions that support the literary disciplines in their conventional form has proved fundamental. Modes and categories inherited from the past no longer seem to fit the reality experienced by a new generation.

New Accents is intended as a positive response to the initiative offered by such a situation. Each volume in the series will seek to encourage rather than resist the process of change; to stretch rather than reinforce the boundaries that currently define literature and its academic study.

Some important areas of interest immediately present themselves. In various parts of the world, new methods of analysis have been developed whose conclusions reveal the limitations of the Anglo-American outlook we inherit. New concepts of literary forms and modes have been proposed; new notions of the nature of literature itself and of how it communicates are current; new views of literature's role in relation to society flourish. *New Accents* will aim to expound and comment upon the most notable of these.

In the broad field of the study of human communication, more and more emphasis has been placed upon the nature and function of the new electronic media. *New Accents* will try to identify and discuss the challenge these offer to our traditional modes of critical response.

The same interest in communication suggests that the series should also concern itself with those wider anthropological and sociological areas of investigation which have begun to involve scrutiny of the nature of art itself and of its relation to our whole way of life. And this will ultimately require attention to be focused on some of those activities which in our society have hitherto been excluded from the prestigious realms of Culture. The disturbing realignment of values involved and the disconcerting nature of the pressures that work to bring it about both constitute areas that *New Accents* will seek to explore.

Finally, as its title suggests, one aspect of *New Accents* will be firmly located in contemporary approaches to language, and a continuing concern of the series will be to examine the extent to which relevant branches of linguistic studies can illuminate specific literary areas. The volumes with this particular interest will nevertheless presume no prior technical knowledge on the part of their readers, and will aim to rehearse the linguistics appropriate to the matter in hand, rather than to embark on general theoretical matters.

Each volume in the series will attempt an objective exposition of significant developments in its field up to the present as well as an account of its author's own views of the matter. Each will culminate in an informative bibliography as a guide to further study. And, while each will be primarily concerned with matters relevant to its own specific interests, we can hope that a kind of conversation will be heard to develop between them; one whose accents may perhaps suggest the distinctive discourse of the future.

TERENCE HAWKES

Introduction

'Superstructuralism'. I coin the term to cover the whole field of Structuralists, Semioticians, Althusserian Marxists, Foucaultians, Post-Structuralists, etc. 'Structuralism' alone has become too narrow a term for dealing with writers like Foucault, who violently resent being called Structuralists, or like Derrida, who define their position explicitly in opposition to Structuralists. The term 'Structuralism' is better reserved for writers such as Saussure, Jakobson, Lévi-Strauss, Greimas and Barthes (the Barthes of *Elements of Semiology* and *Mythologies* and *The Fashion System*), who share a characteristic way of thinking about *structures*. In relation to 'Structuralism', 'Superstructuralism' appears as '*super*-Structuralism', a larger intellectual phenomenon over and above Structuralism (taking 'super' in its strict Latinate meaning). 'Superstructuralism' in this sense serves to give us our bearings by reference to an already established terminology.

However, 'Superstructuralism' can also be read in another and more important sense, as '*superstructure*-alism'. For one of the things that Structuralists, Semioticians, Althusserian Marxists, Foucaultians and Post-Structuralists share is a certain characteristic way of thinking about *superstructures*. To put it roughly, the Superstructuralists invert our ordinary base-and-superstructure models until what we used to think of as superstructural actually takes precedence over what we used to think of as basic. In this respect, Superstructuralism represents what Foucault (in any case other than his own) would call an *epistēmē* – an underlying framework of approach and assumption. Even when Derrida refutes Lévi-Strauss or Baudrillard declares war on Foucault, the hostilities are still conducted over a common ground.

But this does not mean that there is a simple centralized unity to the Superstructuralist epistēmē. I do not want to suggest that Superstructuralism can be focused upon a single central text, or moment, or programme. To do Superstructuralism justice, we must grasp it as a complex multiplicity, as a whole with many parts. And, in looking for connections between the parts, we must be careful never to collapse them merely one into another.

The most obvious distinction to be drawn within Superstructuralism is the distinction between the Structuralists and the Post-Structuralists. The Structuralists, as I have described them, are those who share a characteristic way of thinking about structures: Structural Linguists like Saussure and Jakobson, Structural Anthropologists like Lévi-Strauss, and Structuralist Semioticians like Greimas and Barthes. (Most self-styled Semioticians can be classed as Structuralists from this point of view, with the notable exception of Julia Kristeva.) Of course, there is also a chronological progression from the earlier Structuralists, who work within specific disciplines, to the later Semioticians, who proclaim a single overarching study of culture as a whole. But the characteristic way of thinking about structures remains essentially the same, as does the characteristic scientific orientation. The Structuralists, in general, are concerned to *know* the (human) world – to uncover it through detailed observational analysis and to map it out under extended explicatory grids. Their stance is still the traditional scientific stance of Objectivity, their goal the traditional scientific goal of Truth.

The Post-Structuralists are a very different kettle of fish. The Post-Structuralists fall into three main groups: the *Tel Quel* group of Derrida, Kristeva and the later Barthes (the Barthes of *The Pleasure of the Text*, 'Change the Object Itself' and 'From Work to Text'); Deleuze and Guattari and the later Foucault (the Foucault of *Discipline and Punish* and *The History of Sexuality*,

Vol. 1); and (on his own) Baudrillard. Compared to the Structuralists, who possess a certain spirit of scientific co-operation (even to the extent of sacrificing coherence for comprehensiveness, like Eco in his *Theory of Semiotics*), these groups are fractious in the extreme, and make the most of their differences. None the less, they do share a characteristic new philosophical position (as we shall see in Part Three) – and this characteristic new philosophical position is not only incompatible with the concept of structure but also quite radically anti-scientific. In effect, the Post-Structuralists bend the philosophical implications of the Superstructuralist way of thinking about superstructures back round against the traditional stance of Objectivity and the traditional goal of Truth. And, with the destruction of Objectivity and Truth, scientific *knowledge* becomes less valuable than literary or political *activity*; and detailed observational analysis and extended explicatory grids are discarded in favour of instantaneous lightning-flashes of paradoxical illumination.

But this distinction between Structuralism and Post-Structuralism still fails to account for three major independent figures: Althusser, Lacan and the earlier Foucault (the Foucault of *Madness and Civilization, The Birth of the Clinic, The Order of Things* and *The Archaeology of Knowledge*). None of the three can be regarded as either simply a Structuralist or a Post-Structuralist. On the one hand, they do not share the Structuralist way of thinking about structures, they challenge Objectivity and Truth, and they introduce the characteristic Post-Structuralist themes of Politics, the Unconscious and History. But on the other hand, they do not share the characteristic new philosophical position of Post-Structuralism, which arrives only with Derrida's crucial new arguments in 1967, and which flourishes only under the new sensibility generated by the Paris student riots of May 1968. Althusser, Lacan and the earlier Foucault thus stand between the two main movements in Superstructuralism – yet they are too important to be given a merely transitional status. We must form a special category for them, and consider them as a movement – or three separate movements – in their own right.

In what follows, then, I shall be trying to give due attention to all these many kinds of Superstructuralism. But I shall at the same time be making certain exclusions. In the first place, I

shall not be talking about 'Structuralism' as Jean Piaget understands the term, in a sense so extended that virtually every
scientist or mathematician who thinks about structures can
claim to be a Structuralist. 'Structuralism', as I have described
it, is a species of 'Superstructuralism'; and not every way of
thinking about structures belongs under 'Superstructuralism'.
The Structuralists have their own special way of thinking about
structures which relates to the fact that they also have their own
special way of thinking about superstructures. And this special
way of thinking about superstructures is fundamentally at odds
with the creative and volitional way of thinking which Piaget
himself promotes in his own structure-oriented psychology.

I shall also not be talking about the spread of Semiotics into
the Anglo-Saxon world. The Anglo-Saxon Semioticians, with
Sebeok as their editorial figurehead, undoubtedly do have a way
of thinking about structures which is under the influence of the
Structuralists' special way of thinking about structures. But this
way of thinking still does not drive out certain underlying
assumptions derived from Anglo-Saxon empiricism. It is here
significant that the Anglo-Saxon Semioticians are equally under
the influence of C. S. Peirce, whose version of semiotics ties in
with a general philosophical position quite alien to the Superstructuralist epistēmē. In fact, it is probably fair to say that
the influence of Superstructuralism upon the Anglo-Saxon
Semioticians is mainly in the area of method and technique.
Compared to the Structuralist Semioticians, the Anglo-Saxon
Semioticians are largely indifferent to matters of philosophy;
their interests are more practical, focusing upon various
specific studies in various specific fields of communication. So
although they certainly keep company with the Structuralist
Semioticians for a while, their contributions are of little
importance relative to the concerns of this book.

My third exclusion is an exclusion within Superstructuralism
itself. I shall not be talking about the Structuralist and Post-
Structuralist varieties of literary criticism. This does not mean
that I consider literary criticism an insignificant or peripheral
domain of Superstructuralism. On the contrary, it is plain that
literary criticism has been the source for many crucial Superstructuralist theories, and a recurring reference point. But
modern literary criticism has a rather special relation to its

subject-matter: that is, it relates primarily to modern literature, to the literature which springs (originally) from the French Symbolist movement of the late nineteenth century. And this literature is precisely such as to require and justify the Superstructuralist way of thinking.[1] It is thus hardly surprising that modern Anglo-Saxon literary criticism, beginning with the New Critics, developed something fairly similar to the Superstructuralist way of thinking long before the arrival of any direct Superstructuralist influence.

However, the example of modern Anglo-Saxon literary criticism also shows how this way of thinking can be quite narrowly confined to a purely literary subject-matter. For the Anglo-Saxon critics, starting with I. A. Richards, typically defined literary language in terms of an opposition to ordinary language – ordinary language as already defined by the Logical Positivists and their ilk. In other words, the Anglo-Saxon critics accepted a referential, denotational language as the norm, and tried to justify literature only as an exceptional case. But with Superstructuralism, the Superstructuralist way of thinking spreads out beyond literature and makes all language non-referential, non-denotational. It is in this wider spread of the Superstructuralist way of thinking that the Anglo-Saxon reader can best appreciate the full size of Superstructuralism's claims.

Part One

The Superstructuralist
way of thinking

Preliminaries

Superstructuralism has its roots in the human sciences. Ultimately it derives from the way in which linguistics and social anthropology were first set up, in France, around the beginning of the twentieth century. At that time, a new kind of fact – the human fact – swam into scientific ken, requiring the development of a new perspective. And this new perspective was no mere extension of the perspective of the natural sciences – though it took fifty years for the true magnitude of the divergence to emerge. Under this new perspective, the human sciences constituted themselves as *unnatural* sciences.

In Part One of this book, I shall be looking at a wide variety of Superstructuralist insights in many diverse fields of human science: in linguistics, anthropology, psychoanalytic theory, political economy and general Semiotics. And I shall be attempting to demonstrate that all these various insights are generated by a special kind of vision – a vision that inverts our ordinary base-and-superstructure models and sees what we used to think of as superstructural as having priority over what we used to think of as basic.

More specifically, I shall be dealing with the two primary forms of such inversion: on the one hand, a priority of Culture over Nature, and on the other hand, a priority of Society over the Individual. Ordinarily we assume that Culture is subsequent to Nature, superimposed upon Nature. But according to the Superstructuralists, Nature is itself only a cultural construct, and a particularly recent one at that. According to the Superstructuralists, Nature was added on to human reality by the seventeenth-century rise of the natural sciences. Similarly, we assume that Society is subsequent to the Individual, arranged between individuals. But according to the Superstructuralists, the Individual Self is only a relatively recent cultural construct, added on to human reality by the seventeenth-century rise of the bourgeois ethic of individualism.

This is a paradoxical way of thinking, and especially paradoxical in relation to Anglo-Saxon ways of thinking. For it is in Anglo-Saxon countries that the natural sciences and the ethic of individualism have been most strongly developed and most fondly taken to heart. And it is in the Anglo-Saxon countries that the assumed priority of Nature and the assumed priority of the Individual have passed over into a kind of plain man's down-to-earth 'common sense'. Anglo-Saxons have the feeling of having their feet very firmly planted when they plant them upon the seemingly solid ground of individual tastes and opinions, or upon the seemingly hard facts of material nature.

In looking at various characteristic Superstructuralist insights, I shall be showing how Superstructuralism refutes this kind of 'common sense'. Indeed, I shall be deliberately drawing attention to the paradoxicality of Superstructuralism in relation to Anglo-Saxon ways of thinking. Most previous Anglo-Saxon accounts have tried to make Superstructuralism accessible to the Anglo-Saxon reader by making it as far as possible familiar. No doubt this was a necessary approach when Superstructuralism was still an unknown commodity. But in the end, such an approach sells Superstructuralism short. In the end, Superstructuralism is important and exciting precisely *because of* the enormous gulf that separates it from Anglo-Saxon ways of thinking. Unfortunately, even the most ardent Anglo-Saxon supporters of Superstructuralism have not always made the leap across the gulf.

Saussure and the concept of 'langue'

(i)

Of all human sciences, linguistics holds a special and central place for Superstructuralists. Superstructuralists share in the common and characteristic view of the twentieth century, that man is to be defined by his outward language rather than by his inward powers of mind. For how could ideas exist in the mind without words? And how could powers of reasoning operate without sentences? Such arguments have long been familiar in the Anglo-Saxon world. Man, it is claimed, has a unique way of thinking essentially because he has a unique instrument with which to do his thinking.

But the Superstructuralist notion of this instrument is none the less very different to the usual Anglo-Saxon notion. The Superstructuralist notion is founded upon the concept of 'langue', as first advanced by Saussure. Saussure considered himself a scientist, and argued, for instance, that the down-to-earth reality of speech should take precedence over the idealized propriety of writing. But at the same time, he argued that 'langue' should take precedence over 'parole', i.e. that the system of language in general should take precedence over the sum total of all the actual utterances ever actually uttered. This is a most surprising argument from the point of view of the *natural* sciences – where the positive physical facts are the only appropriate evidence. But, as Saussure recognized, the positive physical facts are not sufficient to account for language *as language*, as signifying and bearing information.

The well-known chess analogy can help to illuminate Saussure's insight here. At first glance, it seems obvious that one should study chess in terms of the sum total of all the moves in all the games that have ever actually been played. But one will fail to account for chess *as a game* unless one also understands that every actual move is selected from a much larger range of possible moves. To study chess properly, one must look at the simultaneous system of principles for making moves, the simultaneous system which implicitly lies behind every move at every single moment of the game. And this system precedes any actual moves – at least in so far as the player must have it already internalized before he can even begin to play.

Similarly with language. The system of 'langue' precedes any actual utterances – at least in so far as the speaker must have it already internalized before he can even begin to speak. A speaker who knows how to speak only those words which he actually does speak can hardly be using language to signify or bear information. His utterance would be more in the nature of a bird-call. As modern information theory shows, the informational value of a given signal is directly proportional to the range of possible signals that have *not* been selected. To account for language properly, one must understand the simultaneous system of 'langue', the simultaneous system which implicitly lies behind every word at every single moment of utterance.

Of course, it is not only the speaker but also the listener who must have the system of 'langue' already internalized. 'Langue' must always be shared – and shared, ultimately, by a whole society. No single person can create new words and meanings. As Saussure puts it: '[langue] is the social side of speech, outside the individual who can never create or modify it by himself; it exists only by virtue of a sort of contract signed by the members of the community'.[1]

The special feature of this 'contract' is that no one ever gets the chance to evaluate it before signing. The individual absorbs language before he can think for himself: indeed, the absorption of language is the very condition of being able to think for himself. The individual can reject particular knowledges that society explicitly teaches him, he can throw off particular beliefs that society forcibly imposes upon him – but he has always already accepted the words and meanings through which such knowledges and beliefs were communicated to him. Words and meanings have been deposited in the individual's brain below the level of conscious ownership and mastery. They lie within him like an undigested piece of society.

In one obvious respect, there would be no point in wanting to evaluate the 'contract' anyway. There would be no point in wanting to decide whether a particular signifying sound was or was not appropriate to the particular thing signified. For, except in rare cases of true onomatopoeia, the relation between signified and signifier is always equally unmotivated and always equally inappropriate. To object to the way in which the sound 'd-o-g' is linked to a specific kind of quadruped would be as absurd as objecting to the way in which the pawn in chess is linked to a particular kind of move. There simply is no natural relation against which the sign-relation might be evaluated. Language is thus on the one hand necessary (the language-user must accept it as it is) and on the other hand arbitrary (it could have been quite otherwise). In a single word, language is conventional.

(ii)

The concept of 'langue' leads on almost inevitably to the concept of what Saussure called 'value' – and what I shall here call 'differentiation'. For if language as signifying depends upon the selection of one linguistic item as against other possible items, then language as signifying depends not upon the particular positive properties of what is uttered but upon the formal difference between what is uttered and what is *not* uttered. Thus a sentence spoken in a loud voice or written in a neat handwriting does not carry any more information than the same sentence spoken in a soft voice (as long as that voice is audible) or written in a sloppy handwriting (as long as that handwriting is legible). In the business of signifying, what matters is that the same structure of formal relations is preserved. What matters is that a sloppily written 'a' stands in the same relation to a sloppily written 'b' as a neatly written 'a' to a neatly written 'b' – and in the same relation as a (loudly or softly) spoken 'a' to a (loudly or softly) spoken 'b'. The equivalence between the various marks and sounds that can represent an 'a' does not depend upon any simple physical similarity, but upon the equivalent position which these marks and sounds occupy within their respective systems.

Again, the chess analogy can be illuminting. Here too, the particular material properties of the chess-board and pieces are in certain respects irrelevant. When chess is played by correspondence, for example, one player may make his moves on a massive board with wooden pieces, the other may make his moves on a travelling set with plastic pieces, and both will presumably write down their moves in the standard symbolic notation, $Q4$ to $K5$, etc. Yet *as a game* it is still all one and the same. To think chess *as a game* is to think the board and the pieces formally, abstracting away from their full individual thingishness, their *quidditas*.

Such abstract thinking works by a setting up of absolute discontinuities. In the world of things, a chess-piece never sits exactly in the centre of a square, it is always more towards one side or another. It may even overlap on to a neighbouring square. But none of this matters in chess as a game. In the game, a piece is simply and wholly on one square until it overlaps so far as to be simply and wholly on another square. There are no degrees of on-ness, no transitions between squares. The board is differentiated out into sixty-four perfectly discrete categories of space.

Similarly in the case of language. Signifiers, for instance, are visible marks and audible sounds – but not on the same level as ordinary non-signifying sights and sounds. The divergence of level is evidenced by the way in which we manage to hear a softly spoken phrase over and above a much greater volume of non-signifying noise. The phrase we hear is a formal pattern of sounds differentiated into discrete categories. And, as Saussure points out, the actual sounds may vary considerably within their categories:

In French, for instance, general use of a dorsal *r* does not prevent many speakers from using a tongue-tip trill; language is not in the least disturbed by it; language requires only that the sound be different and not, as one might imagine, that it have an invariable quality.[2]

Every voice has its own particular properties. A phrase may be uttered rapidly or laboriously, gruffly or gushingly, in a local accent or through a distorting microphone: provided that the shift is consistent, we can soon adjust to the unfamiliarity of each individual phonetic item. What matters is that the overall system of differences be preserved: 'The important thing in the word is not the sound alone but the phonic differences that make it possible to distinguish this word from all others.'[3]

Conversely, when the overall system is not preserved, our habits of hearing will actually prevent us from adjusting to the new differences. The French speaker who has always heard a single category of *r* in the dorsal and tongue-trilled pronunciations will find it very difficult to recognize what is going on in a languge where the difference between these two sounds is significant. Similarly, the English speaker who has always heard a single category of *th* in 'that' and 'thief' will find it very difficult to recognize what is going on in a language where the difference between these two sounds is significant. The differences, in both cases, are quite glaring; but we overleap them so automatically that only a special effort of retraining can recover them. The particular categories of our own linguistic system are so deeply ingrained that we never really hear the full individual sound at all.

The principle of differentiation applies no less to signifieds. Signifieds are concepts – but not in the way that we ordinarily think of concepts. Saussure's way of thinking of concepts has nothing to do with images or mirrorings or mental 'things' of any kind: 'The concepts are purely differential and defined not by their positive content but negatively by their relations with the other terms of the system. Their most precise characteristic is in being what the others are not.'[4] Such concepts are like holes in a net: specified by their boundaries but empty in themselves.

Consider the concept signified by the word 'rape'. Evidently it is a concept that leads to some very strong feelings. And yet, in itself, it is curiously empty – as though the very abomination of the word deflected one's thinking away from the reality of rapes, as though the very unity of the word deflected one's thinking away from the very varied and particular ways in which rapes actually happen. Hence the general inability to recognize degrees or transitions in rape: as far as society is concerned, a woman not *simply* raped has not been raped at all. We can conclude that the meaning of 'rape' is not just a particular positive content of the word itself, but depends upon the position of the word in a system which includes such opposing words as 'love' and 'marriage'. What 'marriage' *is* is what 'rape' *is not*: approval and legality polarized against abhorrence and criminality.

The relational character of the meaning of 'rape' has been especially apparent ever since feminists started to insist upon talking about 'rape within marriage'. Why has it proved so difficult to persuade society at large to accept this combination of meaning? Clearly, the reality of sex-by-force may be equally brutal and humiliating inside or outside of marriage. But the meaning of 'rape' cannot be simply referred to reality in this way. It depends upon the institutionalized opposition between the meaning of 'rape' and the meaning of 'marriage'.

The system of meaning-categories that society transmits to successive generations thus exists as an interdependent whole. Change one signified, and the others must change too. As Saussure argues, if the word 'craindre' were dropped out of the French language, the boundaries of neighbouring words like 'avoir peur' would have to shift to incorporate the left-over space. 'Language is a system whose parts can and must all be considered in their synchronic solidarity.'[5]

It is only when one understands this 'synchronic solidarity' that one really understands the meaning of an individual word. A visitor to western society might well learn that 'rape' means sex-by-force, yet never grasp the distinctive character that the word acquires in relation to such other words as 'love' and 'marriage'. Similarly, a visitor *from* western society might well learn that certain words in the language of an Indian tribe mean 'maternal uncle' and 'sister-in-law's brother', yet never grasp the interactions that lock all such family words into a system, and make the meanings meaningful. Truly, the total interdependent system of a society's meaning-categories carries a total interdependent way of looking at the world.

(iii)

This is all very different to the Anglo-Saxon approach to language. The Anglo-Saxon philosophers who first theorized about language (round about the same time as Saussure) sought to raise up the concept of language only in order to put down the concept of mind. Words were to substitute for ideas, but not for particular concrete things. On the contrary, the world of particular concrete things would emerge all the more strongly by this reduction of its old opposite, the world of mind. For Anglo-Saxon philosophers, language philosophy seemed to offer a new way of encompassing the traditional goals of traditional Anglo-Saxon empiricism.

So, from the very first, Logical Atomists and Logical Positivists looked to the referent or 'Bedeutung' of a word. Without referents, language was held to be meaningless. The whole tactic consisted of overleaping the 'Sinn' or signified, and connecting the signifier directly on to the particular concrete thing referred to. Meanings as concepts in the world of mind were rendered redundant; there remained only the world of particular concrete things with particular concrete words attached to them.

In ordinary language, the proper name is the most obvious case of a direct connection between signifier and referent. Names like 'Mary Spraggons' or 'Bluebell' or 'Woolloomooloo' do not work by way of a concept; they point to some particular concrete thing, but they do not say what kind of a thing it is. (Of course, Mary Spraggons is probably human and female, but the name could also be attached to a rose or a boat.) It is therefore hardly surprising that Logical Atomists and Logical Positivists tended to regard proper names as the ideal form of language, underlying all other forms. Bertrand Russell, for instance, thought that a word like 'sailor' could and should be itemized, in theory at least, into all the names of all the individuals who are or have been sailors: 'Henry Smith', 'Jacques Dubois', 'Horatio Nelson' . . . and so on, *ad nauseam*.[6] In effect, a general category of conceptual meaning could and should be rewritten as an accumulation of particular pointings without conceptual meaning.

Pointing in single names leads on to assertion in whole

sentences. In true or false arrangements of names, language as assertion matches up directly against the world of particular concrete things. Again, it is hardly surprising that Logical Atomists and Logical Positivists tended to regard assertion as an ideal mode underlying all sentences. And again, Bertrand Russell provided an appropriate rewriting technique, in his seminal Theory of Descriptions.[7] For what happens when 'The present king of France is bald' is rewritten as 'There is one person and one person only who is the present king of France, and that person is bald'? In the original sentence, there is an assumption as to the present existence of a king of France. But in the rewritten version, this assumption has been mastered and made conscious and turned into explicit assertion. In effect, the amount of assertion has been increased, and the amount of assumption decreased.

Alas, the Anglo-Saxon approach to language is hopelessly one-sided. Thus, the sentence-rewriting technique falls foul of the fact that an assertion always ultimately depends upon *some* level of shared assumption between utterer and receivers. Russell may remove the assumption that there is a presently-existing king of France, but the assumption that there is such a thing as being a king still remains. Saussure supplies the necessary antidote here, with his emphasis upon the social side of language. In Saussure's theory, language is constantly and secretly slipping into our minds a whole universe of assumption that will never come to judgment. And the Superstructuralists after Saussure are interested in exactly such assumptions as the assumption that there is such a thing as being a king. Under Superstructuralist analysis, it is the amount of assumption that is increased, and the amount of assertion that is decreased.

As for the word-rewriting technique, the problem arises that, unlike proper names, general categories of conceptual meaning apply in varying degrees and at various times. Many people are 'sailors' for one day of the week, and most people are 'sailors' once in a lifetime. Saussure supplies the necessary antidote, with his principle of differentiation. By the principle of differentiation, a general category of conceptual meaning must be described in terms of its outside boundaries, rather than in terms of its contents, the particular individuals that it has accumulated within. Later Superstructuralists, notably Lévi-

Strauss, Eco and Derrida, have even tried to turn the tables and prove that proper names themselves are really general categories of conceptual meaning.[8]

As for the general tactic of overleaping signifieds and connecting signifiers directly on to referents, this appears plausible only so long as one is looking at language in terms of 'parole'. Only when language comes to actual utterance can the word 'dog' start pointing to this dog or that dog, or some dogs, or every dog. But Saussure's concept of 'langue' establishes a whole realm where words have not yet started pointing at all. In 'langue', the word 'dog' is no more than a potential, a possibility of dogs. Of Frege's two types of meaning, 'Sinn' is to be found in 'langue', but 'Bedeutung' is not. Saussure's twofold distinction of signifier and signified is important precisely in respect of what it leaves out.[9] And even when the most recent Superstructuralists, the Post-Structuralists, propose to dispense with signifieds too, they are still moving in the same direction: not back towards the world of referents, but towards a world composed of nothing but signifiers.[10]

Of course, the Anglo-Saxon approach to language has also changed a great deal since the beginning of the twentieth century, especially since Ordinary Language Philosophy overtook Logical Atomism and Logical Positivism. The relationship between Superstructuralism and Ordinary Language Philosophy is a complicated business, and I shall not attempt to tease out its complications here. Suffice it to say that Ordinary Language Philosophers have shifted the focus on to operational uses of words in particular concrete situations, and away from names and assertions and the reflection in words of particular concrete things – yet this new focus leaves language as firmly embedded in the particular concrete world as ever. Although language is no longer required to *reflect* truly, it is still required to *operate* truly. Ordinary Language Philosophers are just as eager as their forebears to shoot down the metaphysical illusions supposedly created by language that rises above its proper station in the particular concrete world. And such an approach is as far away from Saussure as ever. For, as we shall see, Saussure's approach ultimately heads in the direction of *embedding the particular concrete world in language*.

2

From Durkheim to Lévi-Strauss

(i)

Whereas Saussure is universally recognized as father figure to the Superstructuralist movement, Durkheim's co-paternity has been largely forgotten. Partly, no doubt, it is the fault of his old-fashioned politics, his curiously conservative brand of 'socialisme', which actually lies closer to Mussolini's syndicalism than to any revolutionary brand of socialism. Yet the French tradition of social anthropology founded by Durkheim *was* revolutionary; and Durkheim was not unaware of its revolutionary potential. Above all, his attacks upon the concept of the individual self led the way for later Superstructuralists. 'Individuals are far more a product of common life than its determinant.'[1] According to Durkheim, the concept of the individual self is a relatively recent and relatively superficial arrival in human history.

Founding explanation upon common life rather than upon individuals, Durkheim views society as something much more than the aggregate of its members. He argues for the existence of 'collective representations' which, as generated by man-in-association, are quite different in kind to the individual representations generated by individual men.

Collective representations are exterior to individual minds ... they do not derive from them as such but from the

association of minds, which is a very different thing . . .
private sentiments do not become social except by combination under the action of the *sui generis* forces developed in
association . . . *they become something else* . . .[2]

Such claims fly in the face of common sense, no doubt. How can
mental representations survive *exterior* to individual minds? In
what medium can ideas, beliefs and feelings reside, if not in
individual brains in individual bodies? But common sense has
its limitations; and its limitations soon start to show themselves
when one attempts to trace all social phenomena back to
individual origins.

Consider a simple social group, a teenage gang. What happens when a particular milk-bar suddenly becomes an 'in' place
for the gang to hang out at? Can we really reduce the
phenomenon of 'in'-ness to an aggregate of individual likings
and judgments? Is it not more often the case that members of the
gang like the milk-bar because it is 'in', rather than the other
way around? Does there even have to be one member who
originally likes the milk-bar purely on his own behalf? It would
certainly be very difficult to pin down any such original source.
It seems rather as if everyone catches the feeling of liking from
everyone else, before ever coming to an individual judgment on
the matter at all. The feeling may ultimately reside in individual
brains, but it is never individually generated in the way that we
ordinarily assume. To put it briefly: a milk-bar is not 'in'
because everyone likes it, but because *everyone else* likes it.

Durkheim's own best-known example of a 'collective representation' is the phenomenon of religious belief. Previous
anthropologists, mainly Anglo-Saxon, had attempted to trace
religious belief back to individual origins, back to pre-scientific
misinterpretations of experience that a single human being
might fall into on his own. Tylor and Spencer, for instance, had
suggested that primitive man, remembering dreams in which he
and his fellows live lives detached from their ordinary waking
bodies, might come to believe in the existence of personal
free-ranging spirits; Muller and Jevons had suggested that
primitive man, impressed by the mighty forces of storm, fire,
etc., and inclined to describe all forces in human terms, might
come to ascribe god-like powers to Nature; and Frazer and Boas

had suggested that primitive man, unable to distinguish relations of similarity and contiguity from relations of real causality,
might come to develop purely superstitious systems of ritual
magic as a means of protection in a frightening world. Against
these theories, Durkheim argues that primitive man thinks
more in terms of impersonal forces than personal spirits; that
such forces dwell as readily in grass seeds or human hair as in
grand Romantic storms and fires; and that individualistic
self-serving magic is an offshoot of social religion rather than the
other way around. In general, the forms of religious belief that
these theories take as elementary are in fact later and more
sophisticated derivations.

Durkheim's own definition of elementary religious belief
determines the whole course of his argument, and the whole
course of Structuralist Anthropology after him. According to
Durkheim, religious belief begins with a division between the
sacred and the profane. It does not matter whether the sacred is
thought of as supernatural in the modern sense, nor even
whether it is thought of as higher or transcending. What matters
is not the sacred in itself at all, but the division which differentiates it from the profane: 'The real characteristic of religious
phenomena is that they always suppose a bipartite division of
the whole universe, known and knowable, into two classes
which embrace all that exists, but which radically exclude each
other.'[3] What matters is that the sacred is thought of as a *world
apart*.

Such a definition leads inevitably to totemism as the
elementary form of religious belief. Durkheim takes his
examples of totemism from the Aboriginal tribes of Australia,
though the practice of totemism is common to virtually all
primitive societies. In totemism, each clan within the tribe
holds certain things sacred, and maintains with these things
certain special – and unnatural – relations. Members of an Emu
clan, for instance, will usually be prohibited from eating the
flesh of emus; at the same time, they may be the only clan
permitted to hunt and kill emus. It is thus that Durkheim
explains the complex systems of taboos and interdictions so
prevalent in primitive societies: taboos and interdictions maintain the *difference* of the sacred, and keep it apart from the
profane.

There is an analogy here, albeit remote, albeit humble, with the case of the teenage gang and the milk-bar. For, as we have seen, the 'in'-ness of the milk-bar cannot be defined merely in terms of the likeable properties of the milk-bar as a place in itself. The 'in'-ness of this place depends upon the 'out'-ness of other places, upon a general bipartite division that the gang observes and maintains (at any given time) between what's 'in' and what's 'out'. And, precisely by observing and maintaining its own special division between what's 'in' and what's 'out', the gang draws together and distinguishes itself from the rest of society. The gang is the unity of all those who see the world in the same way. (Note, incidentally, how often such special divisions are expressed in special oppositional terms: 'unreal' versus 'heavy', 'choice' versus 'slack', etc. It seems that every group – or every generation at least – finds it necessary to coin its own new words for its own new sense of what's 'in' and what's 'out'.)

Similarly with the totem-clan. By observing and maintaining its own special division between the sacred and the profane, the clan draws together and distinguishes itself from the rest of the tribe. The clan is the unity of all those who experience the world in the same way. And Durkheim, revolutionizing the apparent order of things, therefore claims that the division between the sacred and the profane actually exists *for the sake of* the unity of the clan. The need for social bonding is the motive behind the whole totemic system. A clan maintains its own special division between the sacred and the profane because that division maintains the clan. Ultimately, totemism is not a matter of man's relation to the natural world at all, even though it directs religious feelings towards plants and animals (both the particular totem-plant or -animal which the clan worships, and the many associated species which the clan holds sacred). Totemism is a matter of man's relation to man. So, when members of the clan worship the clan's particular totem-plant or -animal, they are in fact submitting to the social principle by which they, as individuals, are bonded. 'The god of the clan, the totemic principle, can . . . be nothing else than the clan itself, personified and represented to the imagination under the visible form of the animal or vegetable which serves as totem.'[4] The totem is the clan's own sign of itself.

Yet the clan does not know that the totem is its own sign of itself. The emu's sacredness is experienced as a property of the external world, just like the emu's running speed or feeding habits. Hence the characteristically Superstructuralist paradox. A totemic system is created by man and for man – yet it escapes the consciousness and control of any individual man. It belongs to man-in-association; and individual men are constrained by it in much the same way as they are constrained by the properties of the external world.

(ii)

The more revolutionary implications of Durkheim's social anthropology lay for a long while dormant. In truth, there was always something embarrassingly mystical about Durkheim's conception of 'collective representations'. For, in spite of all qualifications, Durkheim did ultimately believe in a kind of social super-mind, hovering over and above the thinking of individual minds in the same way that the thinking of an individual mind hovers over and above the individual neural elements of the brain. But such super-minds belong less to the realm of science than to the realm of science fiction. Durkheim envisaged an analogy between the unity of society and the unity of the thinking of an individual mind; before Structural Anthropology proper could arise, this analogy had to be superseded.

Even in the interpretation of totemism, one can observe a highly questionable shift in the argument as Durkheim strives to apply his analogy. The shift takes place in Chapter VI of *The Elementary Forms of the Religious Life*, when Durkheim suddenly announces the existence of a single fundamental totem-principle behind the very different totem-plants and -animals that the different clans worship. This allows him to transpose his terms from the clan to the tribe, whilst escaping the seemingly inevitable consequence of his own argument – viz., that the totemic system, by heightening each clan's sense of its difference from other clans, would unify the clan only at the expense of the unity of the tribe as a whole. By introducing a single fundamental totem-principle, Durkheim manages to claim that the general principle unifies the tribe in the same way and at the same time as the particular totem-plant or -animal unifies the clan. He even goes on to derive from the totemic system the later development of the idea of a single God, and the later development of large-scale modern societies as unified by the idea of a single God.

Unfortunately, there is really no reason to suppose the existence of a single fundamental totem-principle. After all, it was Durkheim who, with especial reference to totemism, originally insisted that:

> A religion . . . does not proceed from one unique principle which, though varying according to the circumstances under which it is applied, is nevertheless at bottom always the same; it is rather a whole made up of distinct and relatively individualized parts.[5]

In studying totemism, the anthropologist quite properly tries to extract a general principle from the variety of particular totem-plants and -animals; but there is no evidence that a general principle is what primitive man *himself* worships.

With the advent of Lévi-Strauss, the analogy between the unity of society and the unity of the thinking of an individual mind is superseded. This 'inconstant disciple' of Durkheim (as he calls himself in the epigraph to *Structural Anthropology*) explains social unity in terms of communication. No longer is it a matter of some single principle to which the members of the tribe all adhere, as to a single centre; rather, the members of the tribe are bonded together by a perpetual weave and shuttle of back-and-forth transactions. With the advent of Lévi-Strauss, unity is no longer linked to centralization.

This new attitude first appears in Lévi-Strauss's theory of kinship relations. There are hints towards such a theory in earlier French anthropologists: thus Durkheim had already pointed to the crucial distinction between cultural kinship and biological consanguinity, and Marcel Mauss had already pointed to the element of exchange involved in exogamy (i.e. the 'marrying out' of women to men other than those in their immediate family).[6] But Lévi-Strauss gives the argument a whole new twist when he views kinship exchange as a system of *communication*. And although the detail of his overly neat patterning of kinship relations has been challenged to some effect by

Anglo-Saxon anthropologists, yet his general approach still carries conviction.

According to Lévi-Strauss, 'Exchange – and consequently the rule of exogamy which expresses it – . . . provides the means of binding men together, and of superimposing upon the natural links of family the henceforth artificial rules . . . of alliance governed by rule.'[7] Earlier anthropologists such as Radcliffe-Brown had sought to found kinship relations upon the biological family unit, upon the relations of husband to wife, brother to sister, and father to son. But they could not account for the remarkable role of the 'maternal uncle' in primitive societies, that is, the uncle on the mother's side, whose relation to the child seems often almost as important as the father's. Lévi-Strauss, arguing from Radcliffe-Brown's evidence, even demonstrates a kind of interchangeability between father and uncle roles amongst the primitive tribes of South Africa; for in some tribes the uncle is treated with familiarity and the father with respect, whilst in other – sometimes neighbouring – tribes, the uncle is treated with respect and the father with familiarity.[8] Lévi-Strauss therefore dismisses the biological unit in favour of a larger *exchange* unit, which also includes the relation of mother's brother to sister's son. Marriage thus binds together not just a man and a woman, but a man who *gives* a woman and another man who *receives* her. And the exchange does not end with a single transaction, but obligates further reciprocal transactions. As Lévi-Strauss claims, the system of kinship is determined less by relations *within* families than by relations *between* families.

Once again then, culture predominates over nature. Primitive marriage is no closer than modern marriage to a purely biological and reproductive function. Nor is the universal incest taboo to be explained as a genetic and evolutionary necessity imprinted in the instincts. According to Lévi-Strauss, the necessity which motivates the incest taboo is exactly the same necessity which motivates the role of the maternal uncle: the necessity for exchange and bonding between individuals and families, the necessity for society itself.

Exogamy very commonly takes the form of an exchange of women between clans. Women must marry outside their own clan, and their passage from one clan to another weaves a pattern of reciprocal obligations, often of quite staggering complexity. In effect, one clan needs what another clan has, and vice versa. Thus the totemic system creates interdependences precisely by creating differences. No matter how arbitrary and artificial the separation into clans may seem in itself, it serves to bring about social exchange.

As with women, so with food and artifacts. Following up his theory of kinship with a theory of totemic classification in general, Lévi-Strauss extends the same argument to account for the way in which primitive tribes also classify the non-human objects of the universe into clans. The Emu clan, for instance, may contain not only emus and certain human beings, but also certain stars, certain species of tree, certain species of snake, certain geographical sites – in short, a whole segment of the universe. And, as we have already seen, the human beings in the clan will have special rights and privileges over their own segment. Thus, members of the Emu clan may be the only members of the tribe permitted to hunt and kill emus; or members of a clan which includes certain seeds may be the only members of the tribe permitted to prepare those seeds for food; or members of a clan which includes bowstrings (nothing too small to escape classification!) may be the only members of the tribe permitted to manufacture bowstrings. In primitive conditions, everyone is potentially the same, everyone has the same capacity to hunt emus, prepare seeds for food, manufacture bowstrings. But men take artificial differences upon themselves; and the result, once again, is interdependence and social exchange.

Of course, the taboos that maintain these differences can prove highly inconvenient. If a man cannot kill an emu for himself, if he has to wait for someone else to prepare his food or manufacture his bowstrings, then clearly his dealings with the world are much less than maximally efficient. But dealings with the world are not everything. However efficient his dealings with the world, an individual man is still, in primitive conditions, the weakest of all creatures. Only man-in-association can survive. The inconvenience of the totemic system is more than compensated for by its less obvious but none the less crucial function: the function of bonding individuals into a society.

There are, of course, other creatures that need society to survive too. Still, human society does have one unique form of social exchange: communication through language. It is this that gives man his special powers and advantages. And, according to Lévi-Strauss, the general system of totemic classification provides the basis for communication through language as well as the basis for more solid forms of exchange.

In his view of communication through language, Lévi-Strauss draws upon the Structural Linguistics of Saussure and Jakobson, and their principle of 'langue' as differentiation. He claims totemic classification as a kind of 'langue' on the grounds that a division of the entire universe into separate clans is a primary act – perhaps *the* primary act – of differentiation. No matter that this classification looks hopelessly muddled to modern eyes: emus lumped together with certain stars, trees, snakes, etc. What matters is that *any* classification lays a grid upon the world, and *any* grid upon the world makes communication possible. As Lévi-Strauss says:

> The existence of differentiating features is of much greater importance than their content. Once in evidence, they form a system which can be employed as a grid is used to decipher a text. . . . The grid makes it possible to introduce divisions, and contrasts, in other words the formal conditions necessary for a significant message to be conveyed.[9]

It is like communicating a description of a room. One thinks of doors and windows and chairs as the 'natural' units of description; but for purposes of communication, one might as well divide the room up by invisible superimposed lines through space, into entirely 'unnatural' units like pieces of a jigsaw puzzle. For purposes of communication, the persons addressed will still be able to decode the description, provided only that they too use the same system of lines for dividing up space.

Lévi-Strauss thus refuses to dismiss the apparent irrationalities of totemic classification as mere pre-scientific mistakes and hallucinations – as though primitive man just let his fears and fancies run away with his perceptions. Like Durkheim, Lévi-Strauss has more respect for primitive man's intelligence than most of his Anglo-Saxon counterparts. He sees totemic classification, not as a case of conceptual understanding over-ruled by subjective emotion, but as a case of a different kind of conceptual understanding, in its own way quite as coolly abstract as any modern calculus. The thinking of primitive man, he maintains, 'proceeds through understanding, not affectivity, with the aid of distinctions and oppositions, not by confusion and participation'.[10] When primitive man lumps certain stars together with emus, or when he identifies himself with an emu, he is not being naive but, on the contrary, highly sophisticated.

He is being sophisticated because he is holding different things together in mind on a *non-perceptual* basis. And this is the foundation of all signs and signification. For what makes the linguistic sign if not a holding together in mind of a sound and sense which bear absolutely no physical resemblance to one another? Similarly with other types of sign, similarly with the red traffic-light which means 'Halt car!' or the ringing bell which means 'Day's work over!' Such sign-identifications do not work by physical resemblance, yet the identification is peculiarly complete and instantaneous: the thought of the signifier cannot be separated from the thought of the signified.

This enables us to explain the way in which a native may identify so completely with his clan-totem. It is not that he *perceives* himself as an emu, but that he *interprets* himself as an emu. And, as in the case of signifier and signified, the interpretation involves positional, not physical, equivalence. The relation between emu-man and witchetty-grub-man becomes equivalent to the relation between emu and witchetty grub. In the words of Lévi-Strauss himself: 'The differences between animals . . . are adopted as emblems by groups of men in order to do away with their own resemblances.'[11] By identifying with the emu, man makes a sign of himself, and enters as such into the discourse of his society.

Still, the totemic kind of sign-system is not wholly on a par with more modern sign-systems. In particular, the totemic sign-system does not work with artificial marks-on-a-page or specially constructed traffic lights, but with real emus, real witchetty grubs, real plants and animals. According to Lévi-Strauss, modern man is like an engineer who spans a creek with specialized bridge-building materials and implements; whereas primitive man is like a makeshift handyman, a *bricoleur*, who does the same job with bits of wooden box, old fence poles, oddments of wire, whatever happens to be available. And, for the job of constructing sign-systems, it is real things in the natural world that happen to be available.

Inevitably this affects primitive man's conception of the natural world. If real things are to be constructed into a sign-system, then real things must conform to the formal and differentiated structure by which sign-systems work. And, in fact, there are many primitive customs and taboos which can be seen as enforcing just such a conformity. Lévi-Strauss points to Hawaiian customs and taboos which prohibit sitting on a pillow, or laying one's head on a seat cushion, or sitting above any receptacle containing food, or covering any receptacle containing food with any object which may have been walked on or sat on.[12] The principle here is that what's above should stay above, and what's below, below. For the sake of his own sign-system, primitive man must stand guard over the boundaries between things.

Primitive man is thus abstract-minded even in his concrete-mindedness. It is true that he cannot hold and fix pure formal concepts on their own; lacking the modern notations, he must hold and fix his formal concepts in terms of the natural world. But this also means that, for him, the natural world is *itself*

(Reproduced courtesy of Christian Trenga, aged 7)

riddled with formalization. In this respect, as Lévi-Strauss says, 'nothing is too abstract for the primitive man'.[13] Primitive man mixes the abstract and the concrete in a way that seems strange to us nowadays; but he certainly does not dwell amongst pure sense-data.

Indeed, even nowadays the mixture should not seem so very strange, when we can observe something quite similar in small children. Consider how a child draws a picture of a human being, as on the opposite page. Such a picture presents a kind of visualized taxonomy: 1 head, 2 eyes, 1 body, 2 legs, 2 arms, 2 sets of 5 fingers. The child has drawn, not what he or she sees, but what he or she knows. The child has drawn formally differentiated conceptual units, enclosed in surrounding separating boundary lines and divided absolutely and unnaturally between the head and the body, the fingers and the arms, etc. Children can be very abstract-minded even in their concrete-mindedness.

There are of course some general philosophical implications here. If even children and primitive natives are in their own ways abstract-minded, then it becomes impossible to suppose, as empiricist philosophers have supposed, that all classifications, categories and concepts are built up from an initial buzzing and blooming confusion of sense-data. It becomes impossible to suppose that human beings observe first and interpret second: on the contrary, interpretation is always there. In the words of Lévi-Strauss:

> Savage thought does not distinguish the moment of observation and that of interpretation any more than, on observing them, one first registers an interlocutor's signs and then tries to understand them: when he speaks the signs expressed carry with them their meaning.[14]

Lévi-Strauss's anthropology leads us towards a philosophy of the *a priori*.

But this *a priori* is not grounded in the genetic and biological constitution of the individual. It is imposed upon the individual by society. So, although the individual interprets personal sensory experience through classifications, categories and concepts, these are not universally given and fixed from birth. A philosophy of the *social a priori* thus avoids the pitfalls which beset innatist philosophies. At the same time, the individual does not have to develop these classifications, categories and concepts out of mere personal sensory experience; thus a philosophy of the *social a priori* also avoids the pitfalls which beset empiricist philosophies. As Durkheim first claimed more than three-quarters of a century ago, a philosophy of the *social a priori* may represent a third way, an alternative to the inevitable dilemma of traditional epistemology. For philosophers, according to Durkheim, have always posed the epistemological question in terms of the individual human mind; but the question can be answered only by looking to *social* classifications, categories and concepts outside the individual human mind.

3
Lacan's Freud

The abstract-mindedness that Lévi-Strauss claims for primitive man, Lacan claims for the Unconscious in all men. The thinking of the Unconscious, like the thinking of primitive man, is no mere welter of concrete images, but a functioning sign-system of empty structural differentiations. In Lacan's famous phrase, '*the unconscious is structured like a language*'.[1]

Such a claim looks very strange when viewed against the interpretation of Freud long popularized in Anglo-Saxon countries. On the Anglo-Saxon interpretation, it seems obvious that an underlying and basic level of the mind like the Unconscious must lie especially close to the underlying and basic instincts or biological needs of the human species. And, since instincts or biological needs are appeased through the senses, it seems obvious that they will be represented to the Unconscious in terms of sensory images, concrete and 'primitive' and pre-conceptual. In other words, the unconscious mind functions like the mind of an animal.

But there is a hidden assumption behind the apparent common sense of this Anglo-Saxon interpretation. There is the hidden assumption that whatever is underlying and basic can only be underlying and basic in the way that biology is underlying and basic. Clearly, the traditional Anglo-Saxon orientation towards the natural sciences and behaviouristic explanation of man has been at work behind the scenes here, preparing a space for the Freudian Unconscious to fall into. Hence the all too easy and automatic mistranslation of 'Trieb' as 'instinct' by Freud's English translators. As Lacan has pointed out, Freud deliberately reserves the word 'Instinkt' for talking about the instincts; when he uses the word 'Trieb', he is talking about psychical drives or pulsions which may be quite unconnected to the instincts. In fact, Freud's Unconscious is never *simply* connected to the instincts; and in his earlier works, *The Interpretation of Dreams*, *The Psychopathology of Everyday Life* and *Jokes and the Unconscious*, it is scarcely connected to the instincts at all.

So, whereas the Anglo-Saxon interpretation draws inspiration mainly from Freud's later works, Lacan's 'return to Freud' is essentially a return to the spirit of the earlier works. Indeed, one of the best ways to understand Lacanian psychoanalysis is to hark back to Freud's original understanding of the Unconscious as revealed (during the period of his collaboration with Breuer) in the phenomena of hypnotism. With the phenomena of hypnotism in mind, we shall no longer find it quite so strange to hear Lacan proclaiming that 'the unconscious is neither primordial nor instinctual; what it knows about the elementary is no more than the elements of the signifier'.[2]

Hypnosis, as used for psychoanalytic purposes, reaches down to the underlying levels of mind below consciousness. Thus the hypnotist can lead the patient to recollect childhood memories which he or she either could not or would not recollect consciously. But how does hypnosis work? Twentieth-century hypnotists no longer believe that concentration-on-an-object is in itself the crucial factor, whether the object be a spot upon the ceiling (as often nowadays) or the hypnotist's own eyes (as in the old mesmeric tradition). Such concentration-on-an-object only serves to reduce the general backdrop of outside stimuli and so render the patient more susceptible to what *is* crucial: the words of the hypnotist. Hypnosis, it is now believed, works primarily by verbal suggestion; and there is a continuum between hypnotic trance (which may itself take effect at many different levels of 'sleep') and waking verbal suggestion (as when the hypnotist tests for susceptibility by suggesting to the patient that his or her clasped hands are locking together and cannot be pulled apart). The Unconscious that hypnosis reveals is an Unconscious that answers to language.

In so far as the Unconscious answers to language, language acquires remarkable powers. This is most evident in the stage exploitation of hypnosis, when the hypnotist induces the victim to eat a lemon by describing it as a sweet and juicy apple. The victim, presumably, does not truly hallucinate the visual image of an apple – after all, he holds and handles the fruit according to its proper shape, without fumbling. But he *interprets* it as an apple, and therefore, in spite of his taste buds, enjoys it as an apple. No longer is interpretation a superstructure founded upon a base of sensory perception; sensory perception has been short-circuited, and the not-so-mere word 'apple' now dominates over the thing perceived.

Nor is this power of language limited to immediate effects. By post-hypnotic suggestion, the hypnotist can bring about long-term restructurings of the Unconscious. In the simple case of a smoking cure, for instance, the hypnotist can implant in the hypnotized patient an interpretative connection between the idea of cigarettes and the idea of nausea, and this connection will henceforth manifest itself whenever the patient is tempted to smoke a cigarette in ordinary non-hypnotized life. Whenever the patient is tempted to smoke a cigarette, the hypnotist's not-so-mere words will 'take over'. Similarly, and more spectacularly, in the case of hypnosis on stage: the hypnotist can implant a connection that will cause the victim, even after 'waking', to bark like a dog whenever somebody whistles.

Such post-hypnotic suggestions operate in exactly the same way as those neurotic symptoms which were the original subject-matter of Freud's psychoanalysis. The neurotic who in his speech stumbles over a particular kind of word, or who reacts with a coughing fit at the sight of a particular colour of hair is also 'taken over' by an implanted interpretative connection. In effect, the neurotic depends upon a myth which speaks to him. And the myth which speaks to him is also the myth which was first spoken to him. Not, perhaps, in quite the simple sense of a hypnotist speaking the myth about cigarettes-and-nausea or whistling-and-barking to him. Yet the myth still comes from outside – it is still, in a more general sense, 'the discourse of the other'.[3] The neurotic symptom reveals the existence of a language which remains forever 'other' to the subject in whom it dwells.

This language quite contradicts the usual notion of language as involving the understanding and consciousness of a subject. This language corresponds to a lapse of consciousness: the Freudian *lapsus* which supervenes at the moment when the neurotic symptom manifests itself. In the case of hypnosis on stage, the victim cannot, even immediately afterwards, remember the moment of barking like a dog. As Lacan says, 'in the hypnotic state verbalization is disassociated from the *prise de conscience*'.[4] The Unconscious works like a language of signifiers without signifieds, marks on the page without meanings behind them. 'This passion of the signifier now becomes a new dimension of the human condition in that it is not only man who speaks, but that in man and through man *it* speaks (ça parle).'[5] The Unconscious works as if by the solid *letter* of language.

Of course, the Unconscious also manifests itself in dreams. At first sight, it may seem rather difficult to apply to dreams the concept of a language-like Unconscious. At first sight, it may seem that dreams, like films, are composed of concrete imagery. But there is something very elusive about this imagery: for instance, how much of it is in colour? If some scenes are undoubtedly in colour, are the other scenes in black-and-white? Or are the other scenes not exactly visualized in full at all? Are the other scenes perhaps more *known* as situations rather than *perceived* as pictures? One *knows* that one has come to meet one's father, one *knows* that some kind of disaster has happened to the train – and one *knows* all this without ever *perceiving* any actual evidence. Is it not true that dreams are forever being 'taken over' by interpretations and compulsions that arise by themselves, quite independently of concrete and visual imagery?

This opens the way for a very different explanation of dreams, an explanation first proposed by Freud himself in *The Interpretation of Dreams*. On Freud's explanation, the symbols and abstractions of the Unconscious are *regressed* to the level of perception in dreaming. Dreaming is like reading a book: the language comes first, and the imagery derives from it. And in dreaming as in reading, the imagery varies greatly in fullness and intensity. But the dreamer, unlike the reader, never actually experiences the language to which he or she is responding. The dreamer, like the neurotic, only ever experiences the *effects* of the language of the Unconscious.

(ii)

The difference between Lacan's Freud and the Anglo-Saxon Freud can be related to the difference between Freud's two main models for the psyche: in his earlier works, the Conscious, Pre-conscious and Unconscious model; and in his later works, the Id, Ego and Super-Ego model. Of course, the Unconscious can be compared to the Id, and the Conscious and Pre-conscious to the Ego – but the comparison does not run very deep. In fact, the two models imply quite different perspectives.

Especially significant is the presence of the Super-Ego in the later model. The Super-Ego represents the morality of society as internalized within the individual, the morality of society which restrains and represses the self-centred demands of the Id. This puts the impact of society back to a relatively late stage of psychic development, and makes it very difficult to conceive of the Id in the way that Lacan conceives of the Unconscious – as 'the discourse of the other'. For in Lacan's conception, the Unconscious is something like the Super-Ego as well as something like the Id.

The concept of a separate Super-Ego has been crucial to the development of Ego-analysis. Ego-analysis is the pre-eminent school of Anglo-Saxon psychiatry, the school of Kris, Hartman, Loewenstein and Anna Freud. The concept of a separate Super-Ego allows the Ego-analysts to think of society's part in the constitution of the subject as relatively superficial, a final superstructural addition on top of the more basic Id and Ego. And this allows them to view the more basic Id and Ego in terms of the individual, founded ultimately upon the individual organism. In the grand old Anglo-Saxon tradition, what's basic is what's individual. And for the Ego-analysts, most of the psyche's problems can be attributed to an overdeveloped Super-Ego repressing natural instincts to an unnecessary degree. An overdeveloped sense of conventional morality denies the truth of the individual.

With the Super-Ego cast in the villain's role, the Ego bids for the role of hero. Compared to the imposed and extraneous Super-Ego, the Ego begins to look like a healthy growth, a natural extension of individual organism, instincts and Id. According to the Ego-analysts, the Ego can actually serve the Id by recognizing possible obstacles to immediate satisfaction and charting a more rational course to long-term satisfaction. Instead of merely blocking off self-interest with morality, the Ego can understand and balance self-interest against the necessary mutual limits of social life. It is for the sake of such understanding that the Ego-analysts encourage the Ego to out-think the Super-Ego and become aware of the true needs of the Id. Once 'out on top', the Ego can supposedly draw all the parts of the individual's psychic system into a coherent working whole.

Ego-analysis is Lacan's favourite *bête noire*. Whereas the term 'Ego' automatically suggests the individual selfhood of 'ego' in the ordinary sense, there is no such suggestion in any term of the Pre-conscious, Conscious and Unconscious model. The sense of being an individual self is unnecessary to the Conscious or Pre-conscious – and downright *untrue* to the Unconscious. For in the Unconscious, as we have seen, society and the 'other' have *already* preceded individuality and the self. Far from being a healthy growth or natural extension, individual selfhood is thus a 'méconnaissance', imposed and extraneous, a paranoid construct. And in the psychoanalytic cure, it is not something to be encouraged but something to be overcome. 'In my experience,' says Lacan, 'the ego represents the centre of all *resistances* to the treatment of symptoms.'[6] For the psychoanalyst, the most common and most troublesome reaction from a patient is 'I can't bear the thought of being freed by anyone other than myself.'[7]

Lacan explains the false construction of the individual self in two stages. The first stage occurs somewhere after the age of six months, when human children first become aware of their own image in a mirror. Other animals react differently to their image in a mirror: cats, for instance, seem unable to recognize the image as their own, while chimpanzees seem to recognize the image as their own but then lose interest in it. Only human children are fascinated with the image precisely *when* they recognize it as their own. And this, according to Lacan, is because the image they recognize as their own is also an image of themselves as they aspire to be. For the image of the physical body as seen in a mirror, as seen from outside and from a distance, is an image of a unified and coherent self clearly separated off from the rest of the world. And human children, because of some human 'prematurity of birth' or 'primordial Discord', long to overcome their own disunity and incoherence by identifying with this image.[8] Like Narcissus, they fall in love with themselves as seen from outside and from a distance, as seen in the gaze of the 'other'.

The second stage occurs from the age of eighteen months on, when the child enters into society and society's language enters into the child. This language phase depends upon the double-sided mechanisms already developed in the mirror phase. On the one side, language belongs to society, and in order to acquire it the child must surrender something of self, must learn to speak from the position of the 'other'. But on the other side, when the child speaks of self from the position of the 'other', this self is more unified and coherent than ever. For to enter into society's language is to enter into a personal name and a personal pronoun; to speak of self in society's language is to speak in terms of 'me', 'myself' and 'I'. The paradox continues as before: the individual self derives not from some real inner sense of self, but from the 'other', from outside.

The case of hypnosis furnishes an excellent illustration of the imposed extraneous nature of the individual self. The stage hypnotist's victim may eat a lemon under the influence of hypnotic suggestion, or may bark like a dog under the influence of post-hypnotic suggestion; yet afterwards he will almost always try to maintain that his behaviour was under his own control. Even when he has been forced to admit to some very odd behaviour indeed, he still feels that he had perfectly sound reasons for it at the time. Frequently he ends up by resorting to blatant evasions or ridiculous excuses and rationalizations. It is as though he must at all costs paper over the cracks and incoherences in his façade of unity.

If the loss of individual selfhood is the ultimate fear, then the confirmation of individual selfhood is the ultimate desire. In Lacanian psychoanalysis, this desire surmounts and wholly dominates over the supposedly 'basic' needs of the organism. Instead of the Ego merely helping the Id to achieve satisfaction in a more rational way, the egotistic sense of being an individual self now produces its own thoroughly irrational kind of desire. Lacan demonstrates this new kind of desire specifically in relation to the language phase. For although the child acquires language in order to request and demand and have 'basic' needs satisfied, yet the very process of acquiring language changes the nature of what's wanted. Desire is not a matter of simple self-interest when spoken in society's language. The child who acquires the 'other' of language acquires the perspective of the 'other' upon 'I'; and, inevitably, 'narcissism envelops the forms of desire'.[9] The mere gratification of warmth and milk and sucking can never suffice; instead the child seeks gratification in and through the perspective of the 'other' upon 'I'. Desire is caught in a multitude of mirrors: desire to take the place of the 'other' in desire (and love and admire 'I' from outside); desire to be what the 'other' desires (as when a woman desires to become the object that a man desires); desire for the object of the other's desire (as when a man desires a woman who is socially designated as desirable). Satisfiable need gets lost in the demand for love and admiration. On this plane, as Lacan says:

> Demand annuls (aufhebt) the particularity of everything that can be granted by transmuting it into a proof of love, and the very satisfactions that it obtains for need are reduced (sich erniedrigt) to the level of being no more than the crushing of the demand of love.[10]

In the end, nothing can ever truly satisfy this new kind of desire.

If human beings are driven by this kind of desire, then they are in a much worse plight than the Ego-analysts recognize. Ego-analysts take a comparatively optimistic view, that only minor and curable maladjustments in the psychic system hinder individuals from attaining the success and happiness they desire. But on Lacan's view, the success and happiness they desire is itself a mirage. He even suggests that this kind of desire is what Freud was trying to grasp in the concept of the Death-drive, the drive towards negativity. Anglo-Saxon Freudians have generally dismissed the mistranslated Death-*instinct* as biologically unworkable. But the negative drive that Lacan associates with ego and 'I' comes not from biology but from culture – and especially western culture. For western culture puts a special emphasis upon individuality and selfhood, and derives therefrom a special dynamism and drivenness. What could be more conducive to expansion and achievement and aggression than a kind of desire that nothing can ever truly satisfy? Lacan turns Freudianism against the very society into which Ego-analysts want their patients to fit.

4
Althusser's Marx

Just as Lacan generalizes and deepens the anti-individualistic implications of Freudian psychoanalysis, so Althusser generalizes and deepens the anti-individualistic implications of Marxist economics. Just as

> Freud has discovered for us that the real subject . . . has not the form of an ego . . . that the human subject is de-centred, constituted by a structure which has no 'centre' . . . except in the imaginary misrecognition of the 'ego', i.e. in the ideological formations in which it 'recognizes' itself

so too

> since Marx, we have known that the human subject, the economic, political or philosophical ego is not the 'centre' of history . . . that history . . . possesses a structure which has no necessary 'centre' except in ideological misrecognition.[1]

In Marx's talk of structures and relations and classes (especially in *Capital*), and in his attack upon the 'Classical' economics of Anglo-Saxon economists like Smith and Ricardo, Althusser discerns a total theoretical revolution.

Marx attacks Classical economics for taking as its starting point the *homo oeconomicus*, the separate human individual as a unit of wealth or labour. According to Smith and Ricardo, economic exchange is motivated by self-interest, whenever two such individuals each need what the other one has; and this kind of barter, multiplied across a whole society, produces the system of free enterprise economy. In a free enterprise economy, human beings come together socially only in order to advance themselves individually – only in order to accumulate *private* possessions.

Althusser widens Marx's attack to take in the whole seventeenth- and eighteenth-century way of thinking that made such a starting point inevitable. For the separate individual was already the starting point in philosophy, history and social theory. The Cartesian philosophy of the *cogito* proclaimed the private 'I think' as the only possible source for truth and explanation after the external phenomena of the world had all been 'doubted' away. The Hobbesian myth of the 'state of nature' hypothesized an original time before the invention of society when men still lived quite separate and alone. And the social theory of Locke and Rousseau sought to re-establish the 'superstructure' of society more closely upon the 'base' of this 'state of nature', with an ideal of elected government and a morality of individual rights and freedoms. Needless to say, the essentially negative 'nightwatchman' role envisaged for such government fitted in perfectly with the system of free enterprise economy.

This way of thinking is still with us. Yet the assumed priority of the individual is no more than assumption; and the myth of the 'state of nature' is demonstrably contrary to the facts. As Althusser remarks, it makes no sense to ask 'how men, whose physical existence, even, always presupposes a minimum of social existence, could have moved from a *zero* state of society to organized social relations'.[2] The seventeenth- and eighteenth-century way of thinking has been undermined by the nineteenth-century discovery of evolution and the twentieth-century discovery of various 'missing links' from man's earliest history. It becomes increasingly obvious that man has always lived in society, as did his primate ancestors before him. And, in the light of recent animal behaviour studies, it becomes increasingly obvious that even primate society is quite amazingly complex, rich and ritualized.

The history of economic exchange has also been traced back to social rather than individual origins. The key figure here is

Marcel Mauss, a follower of Durkheim (but more universally accepted than his master). In *The Gift*, Mauss shows that the earliest form of economic exchange does not operate through barter between two individuals, each in need of what the other one has. The earliest form of economic exchange operates through gifts – the giving of gifts and the social obligation to return gifts with other gifts. Mauss proves the point specifically against Captain James Cook, the eighteenth-century Englishman, who imagined that a few observed instances of barter represented the beginnings of a system of exchange amongst the Polynesians. What Cook failed to observe was the very different gift-and-obligation system of exchange which was *already* in full-scale operation amongst the Polynesians. Similarly in the evolution of most other societies: the gift-and-obligation system appears long before barter between individuals becomes important. Even western society has passed through such a system, during the medieval period of Germanic tribalism and, later, feudalism. In the self-sufficient condition of a technically underdeveloped society, no mere barter for the sake of needs could ever generate the flow of goods that the giving and returning of gifts can generate.

Of course, the gift-and-obligation system looks very odd to us nowadays. Even the medieval period of our own past history seems a kind of unnatural aberration. For we see how the whole system depends upon something quite insubstantial, the idea of being under an obligation to return gifts with other gifts; and we cannot see what there is to stop anyone from just selfishly shrugging the obligation off. By contrast, we see our present-day system as sound and natural, based upon the real substance of solid property that an individual possesses.

But solid property does not count for much if it can be taken away by mere superior fighting force. And in the Middle Ages, the use of mere superior fighting force was still a flourishing practice. Hence the medieval misfortunes of the Jews, whose accumulated goods and wealth were repeatedly and arbitrarily confiscated. In such a period, possession still depended entirely upon the power to enforce possession; and power was not simply a matter of accumulated goods and wealth. A tribal chief or feudal lord was powerful in proportion to the number of men he could call upon to fight for him; which is to say, the number of men he had placed under an obligation to him; which is also to say, the number of men who had received favours or grants or gifts from him. In such a period, there were very sound – and even selfish – reasons for giving away goods and wealth, rather than accumulating them.

Our present-day system is possible only because the threat of mere superior fighting force has been removed. There is no longer the need to prevent fighting by direct social bonding. As Mauss observes, the gift-and-obligation system makes sense when the state of society is the simple sole alternative to the state of conflict. But our present-day system actually incorporates conflict within society. This involves a changed form of conflict, which is now limited to economic competition between individuals. But economic competition between individuals is still incompatible with direct social bonding between individuals. So society has to take a changed form too. In our present-day system, we no longer bond ourselves to particular people on a person-to-person basis, through particular transactions of gift-giving and -receiving. Instead, we bond ourselves to Society as a principle, Society as a whole, Society as founded upon the long-ago transaction of an original social contract. Social bonding now takes a more indirect and impersonal form.

Society as a principle is also, supremely, Society as the Law. Even the myth of the social 'contract' is framed in legal terminology, as Althusser and others have noticed. It is the idea of the Law that keeps conflict within the bounds of economic competition; it is the legal right-of-possession that underlies the substance of solid property that an individual possesses. And, of course, the legal right-of-possession is really just as insubstantial, and just as easy or difficult to shrug off, as is the idea of being under an obligation to return gifts with other gifts. In this respect, our present-day economic system is no more natural or soundly based than the gift-and-obligation system. But our idea of the Law does differ in its abstraction and in the way that it is internalized within each separate individual – so deeply internalized that one seems to obey it more for one's own sake than for anyone else's. In this respect, our present-day system is less overtly – and hence less naturally – unnatural than the gift-and-obligation system. It is hardly surprising that the gift-and-obligation system tends to appear at an earlier stage of society.

Of course, we imagine that we as individuals have freely created Society as a whole, Society as the Law. We imagine that we as individuals have discovered the need to take socially compatible detours towards the satisfaction of our desires – precisely such detours as the Ego, in Ego-analysis, supposedly maps out for the Id. But, on Althusser's view, our freedom as individuals is constructed by society, which enters into us even as it 'liberates' us. Our idea of our own individuality and our idea of Society and the Law are twin-born. *'There are no subjects except by and for their subjection.'*[3] Our idea of our own individuality and our idea of Society and the Law depend upon each other and reflect each other – 'mirror categories' as Althusser calls them.

This is a classic case of polarization, handed down to us from the thinkers of the seventeenth and eighteenth centuries. What is more, it works in the way that polarizations usually work: the two polarized terms define a dimension that excludes all other terms. With the interests of the separate individual on the one side, and the interests of society as a whole on the other, there is no room for the interests of groups and classes that are larger than the individual but smaller than the whole. In our present-day system, specifically, it is unionized labour and political interest groups that are excluded. Thus, the bonding together of individual human units of labour is made to appear factional within society as a whole, and an unnatural surrender of freedom on the part of the separate individual. Individual human units of labour are expected and required to behave *as* individuals. Similarly, the formation of political interest groups is seen as distorting the individual's perception of his or her own separate self-interest, and as disrupting the electoral process which converts the sum total of such self-interests into a disinterested government for society as a whole. Protected by the secrecy of the ballot, individual voters are expected and required to vote *as* individuals. In Rousseau's words, which Althusser quotes, 'It is therefore essential, if the general will is to be able to express itself, that there should be no partial society within the State, and that each citizen should think only his own thoughts.'[4] This is virtually to exclude communication amongst human beings – an extraordinarily unnatural exclusion for a supposedly natural system of government!

The idea of the individual and the concomitant idea of Society as a whole belong to a specific historical phase: the phase of bourgeois ascendancy. It is not surprising that the morality of individual rights and freedoms begins with the Renaissance rise of the Italian merchant class, and becomes dominant, especially in England, during the seventeenth and eighteenth centuries. As Althusser claims, 'this humanist ideology . . . is inseparably linked to the rising bourgeoisie, whose aspirations it expressed'.[5] Individualism is no eternal verity rooted in the depths of human nature, but a comparatively recent phenomenon constructed by a particular kind of society.

(ii)

The notion of individualism as the ideology of the bourgeoisie comes to Althusser from Marx. But ideology for Marx was essentially a matter of explicit ideas and arguments, fed to the working classes in order to persuade them to accept their inferior conditions of existence. For Althusser, on the other hand, ideology is more a matter of the very starting points that are *taken for granted* in formulating explicit ideas and arguments. After all, even the proof of the *cogito* ultimately rests on the ego-centred terms in which Descartes first posed the problem, 'what can *I* know for certain?' This is no longer ideology as 'false consciousness', since it is, according to Althusser, 'profoundly *unconscious*'.[6] What's more, the falsity is no longer on the level of assertions – as in ideas and arguments – but rather on the level of categories – as in the deceptive polarization that divides the human world between the individual and society as a whole. 'It is above all as *structures* that [ideological representations] impose on the vast majority of men.'[7] In short, whereas Marx's ideology functioned as a kind of 'parole', Althusser's functions as a kind of 'langue'.

Ideology on the level of categories is especially difficult to reject, because we do not even know that we are accepting it. And since the world we see is constituted by these categories, there is never any visible mismatch such as occurs on the level of assertion. In particular, the category of our own individual 'I'-hood seems 'a primary "obviousness"'.[8] And, when we look through this category at the world around us, it seems also obvious that our morality should be a morality of individual rights and freedoms, our government an elected government, and our economy a free-enterprise economy. If injustices arise in our social system – well, at least they do not appear to have been *artificially* imposed. If some people are exploited whilst others exploit – well, this must just be the natural way of competition. If there exist enormous differences of wealth and power – well, this must just be a natural consequence of differences in talent and ability. Our social system stands absolved, for our social system is only Nature. And what's the use of blaming Nature?

Herein lies the triumphant manoeuvre of bourgeois ideology. With all questions of social and economic organization shifted out of the realm of politics and into the realm of nature, it becomes impossible to take *political* objection to the *status quo*. Overt repression becomes unnecessary. In our present-day bourgeois system, it is even more obvious than in Marx's time that the working classes are not kept in place simply by the repressive state apparatus of police, army, prisons, courts, etc. Rather, they keep themselves in place: 'the vast majority of (good) subjects work all right "all by themselves"'.[9] The subjection comes from within, from ideology.

At the same time, this ideological manoeuvre is not *deliberately* planned and executed by one class against another. Ideology is as 'profoundly *unconscious*' for the exploiters as the exploited. 'The ruling class,' says Althusser, 'does not maintain with the ruling ideology, which is its own ideology, an external and lucid relation of pure utility and cunning.'[10] The members of the ruling class quite genuinely believe that differences in wealth and power are a natural consequence of differences in talent and ability, and that they themselves started off with just the same individual chance as everyone else. Indeed, it is perhaps by virtue of the especial ardour with which they embrace the principle of the individual that they form themselves *as* a class. As Althusser suggests, 'The ruling ideology is indeed the ideology of the ruling class, and . . . the former serves the latter not only in its rule over the exploited class, *but in its own constitution of itself as the ruling class*.'[11] In other words, ideology serves those who are already its servants.

With all this new depth and importance, ideology has clearly outgrown its old position in the traditional Marxist base-and-

superstructure model. No longer is it merely the surface manifestation of a hidden economic reality. No longer are the
relations of labour and wealth the sole source for the structures
of social power. Ideology as 'langue' represents a new kind of
hidden reality, and an alternative source for the structures of
social power. The notion that all causality begins in the solid
and practical base of the economy is dismissed by Althusser as
crude 'economism'.*

Ideology takes on the crucial causal role especially when
Althusser makes it responsible for reproducing a given power
structure from generation to generation. Althusser suggests that
Marx did not devote much attention to this matter of reproduction, and evidently assumes that, if Marx had devoted attention
to it, he too would have observed ideology's crucial role.[12] But in
Marx's time, in the nineteenth century, there was a much more
obvious way of explaining the reproduction of a power structure
from generation to generation – so obvious that it hardly needed
spelling out. In Marx's time, direct parent-to-child inheritance
of capital was still all-important. Thus the reproduction of the
power structure could be quite satisfactorily accounted for in
solid, practical, economic terms, by the unequal distribution of
inherited wealth. And the bourgeois belief that every individual
starts off with just the same individual chance could be quite
convincingly countered by the reality of capital inheritance –
rather as, in the field of epistemology, the empiricist theory of
the *tabula rasa* might be countered by the reality of biological
inheritance.

In the twentieth century, however, capitalism has entered a
new phase, and the direct parent-to-child inheritance of capital
has become considerably less important. What counts nowadays is not so much the *possession* as the *multiplication* of capital.
Nowadays, the children of the ruling class often carve out their

---

* Of course, Althusser does not wish to set himself against Marx, and so
unearths complexities and contradictions in the original texts to modify the
traditional 'economistic' interpretation. And no doubt the traditional interpretation is an oversimplification, though I suspect that Marx would have
recognized more of himself in it than in the new interpretation. At any rate, I
shall circumspectly refer 'economism' to the traditional interpretation rather
than to Marx himself, at least wherever Marx's own position is in dispute.

own fortunes, without or before or over and above any inherited capital; and, occasionally, so too do the children of the working class. In this more fluid and dynamic phase, individuals can indeed migrate between different classes in the power structure.

What stays the same is the power structure itself. The children of the working class can migrate to the ruling class – but only in so far as they learn the language of power (the language of capital and exploitation and the law). Similarly, the children of barbarians could attain the very highest positions in the Roman Empire – but only in so far as they ceased to think like barbarians, only in so far as they learnt the language of power (the Latin language, to begin with). The differentiation of class positions stays the same, regardless of which particular individuals happen to occupy them. In this way, Althusser allows for a more fluid and dynamic phase of capitalism, yet still counters the bourgeois belief in genuine self-determination. Althusser discloses a third possibility that is neither individualistic nor solidly 'economistic' – rather as Durkheim, in the field of epistemology, discloses a third possibility that is neither empiricist nor biologically innatist.

The Roman analogy also demonstrates the momentum that a self-perpetuating power structure can build up for itself. For even after the 'fall' of the Roman Empire, the Germanic tribes continued to revive and fight over its titles and concepts. In spite of their entirely incompatible social and economic system, the Germanic tribes did not see themselves as destroying the Empire, but only as making a place of their own within it. The Empire had imposed itself so thoroughly upon men's minds that no one could unthink the idea of it. In the same way, ideological 'survivals' from the Czarist regime came to be recognized as a very real problem during the early decades of Soviet rule in Russia. Even though the economic base had been kicked out, the ideological superstructure somehow still remained standing. Althusser sees no way of accounting for such 'survivals' in terms of traditional Marxist 'economism'.[13]

But if it is ideology that perpetuates an existing power structure, then this power structure must be attacked through its ideological apparatuses (school, church, family, literature, sports, the mass media, etc.). 'Ideological State Apparatuses may be not only the *stake*, but also the *site*, of class struggle and often of bitter forms of class struggle.'[14] Revolution depends upon ideological struggle and not just upon economic development – as indeed the history of the twentieth century has already proved. For mere economic development has propelled the most economically developed countries only into a new phase of capitalism; and a comparison of capitalist and communist economies around the world hardly suggests that Marxism will triumph on grounds of sheer economic efficiency. Once again, Althusser takes account of present-day facts that traditional 'economism' can only ignore.

Althusser also avoids the notorious theoretical dilemma of traditional 'economism': if the Marxist state is an inevitable result of economic development anyway, why should one strive to bring it about through political activity? In this respect, traditional 'economism' shifts questions of social and economic organization out of the realm of politics just as does 'Classical' bourgeois theory. For, like Classical bourgeois theory, traditional 'economism' seeks a *natural* base for social and economic organization – in this case, a base of natural economic forces (the inevitable build-up of technology, population, industrialization, etc.). Althusser, on the other hand, views social and economic organization as essentially *unnatural*, that is, as cultural and artificial. What is made by man can also be made *otherwise* by man.

But Althusser does not of course reject economic determinism in order to reintroduce individual free will. It is not individual man who must engage in ideological struggle, but social man, man-in-communication. The existing ideological 'langue' must be opposed by an alternative 'langue' *spoken together* by a group or class against bourgeois society. Which is, after all, the very definition of political activity. For political activity is not merely a matter of thinking revolutionary truths for oneself; political activity requires thinking as a group, sharing a sense of group solidarity. When Nature and the Individual are both ruled out of play, the idea of political activity takes on a new importance. In this respect, Althusser's position marks an inevitable convergence between politics and the Superstructuralist way of thinking. The idea of political activity has indeed taken on a new importance for almost all Superstructuralists following after Althusser.

5
Barthes and Semiotics

(i)

Whereas Althusser reveals the presence of ideologies behind arguments, Roland Barthes reveals the presence of 'mythologies' behind the ordinary everyday things of the world. Even where it seems that things are quite simply perceived without concepts or verbalization, Barthes still manages to demonstrate that cultural interpretations *get their word in* first. The solid world turns out to be not so solid after all.

Consider, with Barthes, the 'mythology' of steak.[1] Is it not true that, when we eat a piece of steak, what we enjoy is not just the material steak itself, but also the *idea* of steak? For steak represents to us a kind of power and heartiness: to eat steak is to eat powerfully and heartily, and to have the feeling of living a powerful and hearty life. Or as Barthes puts it, steak represents to us 'the heart of the meat . . . meat in its pure state', and 'whoever partakes of it assimilates a bull-like strength'.[2] A particular piece of steak has the interpreted cultural 'glamour' of all Steak-hood, long before it comes into contact with the taste-buds. (I use the word 'glamour' with something of the sense that it originally possessed for nineteenth-century Theosophists, the sense of a non-physical aura surrounding a physical body.)

Similarly with wine.[3] Wine is not just a taste but also a visual image (liquid colour, sparkling glass, etc.); and not just a visual image but also an imaginary ambiance (candlelight, sunlit terraces, etc.); and not just an imaginary ambiance but also a whole implied way of life (leisure, chic, style, etc.). Doubtless, the special 'glamour' of wine is not unrelated to its intoxicating effect, yet the 'glamour' itself is almost diametrically opposed to the clumsy and inelegant reality of drunkenness. (Indeed, it is perhaps this peculiar cultural interpretation that keeps drunkenness under control in western societies, and the absence of this interpretation that allows it to wreak such havoc in other societies.) A glass of wine is no mere functional means to an end, but an end in itself – to be dwelt upon and lingered over. Hence the many minor ceremonies that have come to be associated with the drinking of wine: the uncorking, the pouring, the swirling, the sniffing, the manner of holding the glass, and so on. The drinking of wine, even more plainly than the eating of steak, is a ritual. And the purpose of the ritual, as of all rituals, is to make the particular object stand for a general meaning, to make one particular glass of wine stand for the idea of all Wine-i-ness in general.

This kind of 'standing for' is like the 'standing for' by which a word uttered in particular 'parole' invokes the general category of itself in 'langue'. It is not like the 'standing for' by which a signifier, 'd'-'o'-'g', refers across to something entirely different from itself, the signified concept or image of a dog. From wine to Wine-i-ness or from steak to Steak-hood, this kind of 'standing for' rises in level without changing ground. There is no resemblance to the referring or naming or asserting functions of language which Anglo-Saxon language philosophers have deemed crucial. But there is a resemblance to the invocation of 'langue' which Saussure has deemed crucial. With the orientation of language towards 'langue', it becomes possible for Barthes to apply the notion of meaning to vast new territories.

What's more, 'mythological' meanings have a socially unifying effect, as do meanings in 'langue'. For we do not invent the 'glamour' of wine by ourselves, out of our own private memories as individuals; the 'glamour' of wine can only be sustained by a community. Our idea of wine is the idea that it has for others. And to drink this idea is to identify with those others, to commune with that community. Wine here plays the role of a primitive totem – a 'totem-drink' Barthes calls it.[4] In the same way that the clan-totem of the emu unites all those who share and serve its special meaning, so the totem of wine unites all those who share and serve *its* special meaning.

In France, the totem of wine unites all 'true' Frenchmen. Wine-drinking in France is an assertion of the national way of life. As Barthes points out, 'a Frenchman who kept this myth [of wine] at arm's length would expose himself to minor but definite problems of integration'.[5] Similarly, according to Barthes, with steak: in France, steak-eating is thought of as something distinctively French. It is curious that steak-eating is also thought of as something distinctively American in America, and distinctively Australian in Australia!

Conversely, a counter-community typically defines itself by rejecting the dominant totems. From Hippies to Yippies, the members of the Alternative Culture not only turned away from what had been thought of as the American (and Australian, and also presumably French) way of life, but simultaneously developed an aversion to the *meatiness* of steak. The assertion of power and heartiness – and of national power and heartiness – came to seem less appealing in the realm of food just as it came to seem less appealing in the realm of moral values. And although the *penchant* for identifying with man's biological nature remained the same, it was now the eating of vegetables rather than the eating of steak which stood for 'naturalness'. In truth, of course, biology has nothing to do with the eating of *cooked* food in the first place; and certainly cannot explain, in the case of steak, the sudden switch from intense like to intense dislike. Such polarizations are quintessentially cultural.

Subjectively, though, both those who like and those who dislike steak experience their preference as though it came from their own taste-buds. Perhaps I may here be allowed to relate a tale from my own childhood. From the age of about 9 years on, I was convinced that I detested the taste of carrots, and refused to eat the Saturday stew whenever I spotted even the tiniest orange-coloured chunk of carrot in it. I shirked the contradiction when I was told that the other Saturday stews which I did like also contained carrots, but mashed too small for me to see. Not liking carrots was a preference of my own taste-buds, and no one was going to get me out of it! Only now, in my slightly more enlightened maturity, it occurs to me that my detestation of carrots began at the same time as my close friendship with a cousin who already detested carrots. Carrots had a negative meaning for me long before they came into contact with my taste-buds. Not liking carrots was a matter of social solidarity: I belonged to the anti-carrot clan!

The moral of the tale is that subjective conviction is no proof of where a taste really comes from. Of course, we assume that our most immediate tastes must necessarily be our own. In Anglo-Saxon culture especially, we tend to feel suspicious about acquired tastes and cultivated judgments, and correspondingly smug about immediate tastes: 'I like what I like and that's all there is to it.' And, in Anglo-Saxon culture especially, we stand up for our individual right-to-like (or dislike) as though in defence of one of our most fundamental rights as individuals. But our love of our own status as individuals deludes us, and so does our belief in immediate tastes. For Barthesian analysis shows that we can be imposed upon *a priori* as well as *a posteriori*; 'glamours' and 'ideas' can predetermine even the most immediate tastes.

(ii)

In our present century, it has become increasingly important to recognize the kind of meaning that appears in 'glamours' and 'ideas'. For this kind of meaning is now more than just a matter of unconscious person-to-person communication; this kind of meaning is now deliberately *spoken* by advertisers to consumers. In our present century, manufacturers no longer manufacture products alone, but also the needs and desires for those products to satisfy. The new phase of twentieth-century capitalism is also the phase of consumerism.

The new advertising depends very much upon the new technology of visual reproduction. There is an affinity between the camera-picture (whether as photo or filmic sequence) and the kind of meaning that appears in 'glamours' and 'ideas'. Consider Barthes's example of the Panzani advertisement: a photo of a string bag overflowing with tomatoes, onions, capsicums, mushrooms – and, of course, Panzani spaghetti.[6] On the one hand, the things in the photo are presented naturalistically; they are not artificial signifiers referring away to some completely different signified. On the other hand, though, they are presented out of context, detached from the real experience of shopping around markets with a heavily loaded bag, detached from the real chore of peeling, dicing and chopping up vegetables. They are presented for dwelling upon and lingering over, aesthetically. Hence they inevitably tend to become 'glamorized': in this case, into the 'glamour' of the simple peasant-like life and the 'glamour' of what Barthes calls 'Italianicity'. Similarly in the case of a photo of snowcapped mountains or a film of galloping horses. By its very effect of lifting things out of their context, the camera automatically turns them into 'ideas' of themselves.*

So the camera has a double action. It does not simply bring us closer to the real world of things or simply take us away from the human world of meanings. As Barthes says, 'it is not very accurate to talk of a civilization of the image – we are still, and more than ever, a civilization of writing'.[8] After all, it is notable that advertisements invariably put verbal captions to photos or films. The captions may not have the primary role – but they direct and assist and *are on the same level as* the 'glamour' of the photo or the film. It may well be that the new technology of visual reproduction is actually taking us away from the real world of things, by domesticating the real world of things within the human world of meanings.

Armed with the new technology, the twentieth-century advertising industry can effectively intervene in society's system of cultural interpretations. In the case of steak or the case of wine, this intervention is simply an intensification of an existing 'glamour'. Thus, advertisements for wine typically dwell upon images of candlelight or sunlit terraces, with verbal captions suggestive of a chic and leisurely life-style. In other cases,

---

* There is something analogous in the case of a Basque-style house built in the Parisian suburbs. As Barthes points out, a Basque-style house in the Basque country is a necessary product of climate, building materials and the Basque attitude to life; but the Parisian imitation is unnecessary and, to that extent, self-conscious, deliberately asserting its 'Basquity'.[7] Detached from its context, a Basque-style house turns into an 'idea' of itself.

though, a total reorientation may be called for. Margarine, for instance, ordinarily stands for artificial manufacture and an impoverished way of life. In this case, advertisements must either confront the existing 'glamour' directly, with a conversion-story of the kind that Barthes analyses in 'Operation Margarine' (beginning 'A mousse? Made with margarine? Unthinkable!' 'Margarine? Your uncle will be furious!'), or must slide past it indirectly, with an alternative 'glamour' – the softness and smoothness of margarine.[9]

Of course, softness and smoothness would be considered as very secondary qualities in any rational choice of what to spread on one's bread. But there is a 'progress' towards increasingly irrelevant qualities in all advertising. Barthes's study of advertisements for soap powders provides an excellent illustration.[10] Originally, soap powders were given a kind of magical violence, that scoured and purged and even *burnt* the dirt out of clothes: a fantastically intensified 'glamour' which none the less still bore some relation to a practical cleansing action. But more recent advertisements have switched to the quite antithetical 'glamour' of sudsiness. This is a soothing, caressive 'glamour', connoting luxury; the idea of the deepest, whitest, foamingest suds is an idea for wallowing in. But the depth and whiteness of suds has nothing at all to do with any practical cleansing action. The reality of a soap powder's function in the world (an unpleasant reality, connoting drudgery) has been replaced by a fantasy of direct sensuous contact between soap powder and consumer (a fantasy as totally pleasant as it is totally non-functional).

Soap powder advertisements are also revealing in so far as they play upon the consumer's sense of society. In the classic case, a housewife is *initiated* by a friend or friends into the secret of a particular brand of soap powder. The inducement to the consumer here is the inducement to become a member of the clan, to share in the special meaning of the totem. Similarly with all the many advertisements which present a picture of people together *in a group*, sharing (with looks of mutual pleasure and mutual knowledge) a particular brand of margarine, or wine, or whatever. No need to address the consumer in the old straightforward verbal style ('You need . . .', 'The Best Is . . .'). Because our likings are so vulnerable to our impression of what other people like, advertisements can promote the consumption of a given product merely by spreading the impression that it is what other people like. With the aid of the new technology of visual reproduction, the advertising industry can *manufacture society*.

This social aspect does not feature in the attacks upon the advertising industry most commonly heard in Anglo-Saxon countries. The Anglo-Saxon approach is, as always, humanistic and individualistic. Advertisements, it is supposed, undercut the individual's proper freedom to choose by appealing to his or her biological instincts – and most notably, of course, his or her sexual instincts. Barthes's 'mythological' studies reveal the naivety of this approach. For instance, there is nothing biologically basic about the look of the female models pictured in advertisements: nothing biologically basic about the ultra-slim look; nothing biologically basic about the fetishized focusing of (camera) attention upon particular parts of the body (the legs, the bottom, etc.); nothing biologically basic about the way in which different looks go in and out of (photographic) fashion. The female models pictured in advertisements are social signs of sex; as in Lacanian theory, they are desirable as the object of the desire of others. Nor are they desirable only to men. For women identify with these sex-signs, and present-day advertisements for panti-hose are at least as suggestive and seductive as any male-oriented advertisements. The appeal of sex depends upon the special meaning and status that our society attributes to sex. On a Barthesian approach, it becomes clear that the advertising industry is not tapping some basic biological instinct, but merely turning to advantage yet one more cultural 'glamour'.

Once again, then, we find that what appears solid and basic is actually under the power of what appears flimsy and superficial. Once again, we observe the Superstructuralist vision of a superstructure so insidiously vast that it completely surrounds and encompasses its apparent base. And, once again, we confront the Superstructuralist paradox that what springs from human culture can be none the less outside of human will and consciousness. 'Glamours' and 'ideas' have a momentum of their own, it seems, and are quite capable of *Frankenstein-ing* over their creators.

(iii)

This Superstructuralist vision is a harsh and unpalatable vision – much more so than the harsh and unpalatable vision to which scientific positivism has accustomed us. Certainly, the positivist vision, especially in the nineteenth century, showed how human beings are controlled by animal greeds and drives operating from below, rather than by classical conscious Reason operating from above. Certainly, Freud showed the Rationalizations in Reason and Marx showed the False Consciousness in Consciousness. But at least animal greeds and drives still gave one a firm ground under one's feet that one could know and allow for. With Superstructuralism, human beings are controlled once more from above – but not by classical conscious Reason. With Superstructuralism, human beings are controlled by the Rationalizations and False Consciousness which have replaced Reason. A dizzying state of affairs, where one cannot trust one's ideas and yet cannot get down from them either! Compared to this, the security and certainty of the positivist vision begin to look downright attractive.

Indeed, the Superstructuralist vision can undercut the positivist vision precisely in so far as it can expose the 'glamour' of such security and certainty. No one demonstrates it better than Robert Musil, himself an ex-positivist:

Regarding goodness as only a particular form of egotism; relating emotions to internal secretions; asserting that man is eight or nine tenths water; explaining the character's celebrated moral freedom as an automatically evolved philosophical appendix of free trade; reducing beauty to a matter of good digestion and well-developed fat-tissue; reducing procreation and suicide to annual curves, showing what seems to be the result of absolute free will as a matter of compulsion; feeling that ecstasy and mental derangement are akin; putting anus and mouth on one level, as the rectal and oral ends of one and the same thing – such ideas, which, in a manner of speaking, lay bare the sleight of hand in the conjuring trick of human illusion, always meet with something like a prejudice in their favour, which allows them to pass as particularly scientific. Admittedly, it is truth that one so loves here. But all round this shining love is a partiality for disillusion, compulsion, inexorability, cold intimidation and dry reproof, a malicious partiality or at least an involuntary emotional radiation of this kind.[11]

To share the positivist vision is to have the feeling of being initiated into the secret of a special scientists' clan. But it is often little more than metaphoric association that suggests a *hardness* in the facts produced by a *materialism* in the explanation.

Musil's insight, of course, is the insight of a novelist; and it is in literature that one must look for the pre-scientific antecedents of Superstructuralism. For literature is by no means as *soft* as positivists sometimes imagine; literature can create 'glamours', but it can also expose them. French writers, in particular, have a very long tradition of cynical cultural analysis. Their harsh and unpalatable insights into romantic love are characteristic. Thus La Rochefoucauld remarks that 'there are people who would never have fallen in love if they had not heard love spoken about' (*Maxims*, No. 136); Stendhal shows Julien and Mathilde spurred on to passionate behaviour by an 'idea' of love which imposes itself from outside upon their real lack of feeling (*Le Rouge et le noir*); and Flaubert shows Emma Bovary trying to make real-life affairs *stand for* a 'glamour' of exotic romance which she has already acquired from books (*Madame Bovary*). Such insights into *unnaturalness* cannot be reached by starting from the *natural* sciences.

The tradition of cynical cultural analysis attains its greatest heights in *A la recherche du temps perdu*. Proust's world is a world where 'ideas' totally override real things, and, what's more, radically fissure individual personality. In Proust's world, the narrator falls into an 'idea' of love over a mere overheard name ('Gilberte') and a momentary glimpse of girls on bicycles, and his love consistently thrives better upon such signs than upon the full presence of the beloved. In Proust's world, the narrator is captivated by a generalized, glamorized 'idea' of 'Venice-ity', and cannot accept the particular, concrete Venice that he finally, disappointingly, visits. And, in Proust's world, the members of the Verdurins' 'petit clan' share, serve and unite over the 'idea' of Dr Cottard's wittiness, and never find out that Dr Cottard is really not witty in the least. With these and countless other insights in similar vein, Proust should perhaps be ranked with his near contemporaries, Saussure and Durkheim, as one of the father figures of Superstructuralism. Certainly, his imprint is stamped all over Barthes's 'mythological' studies.

But whereas Proust is content to remain at the novelist's level of *ad hoc* insights, Barthes, in his semiological period, aspires to comprehensive systematicity. Barthes wants to be able to deal with Steak-hood or Venice-ity or sudsiness or romantic love, not as they affect one individual mind, but as they affect society in general. He wants to be able to explain our whole modern western society as a single cultural force-field, crisscrossed by meanings and interpretations like a pool of water crisscrossed by waves. In such a field, individual minds are no more than meeting points where waves of meaning intersect. No doubt, the meanings exist only through the varying mental dispositions of individual minds, just as the waves of water exist only through the varying vertical positions of individual water-particles. But individual water-particles do not take part in the horizontal movement of waves, and individual minds do not experience the social movement of meanings. Hence one calculates the varying individual positions or dispositions from an understanding of the larger horizontal or social movements – and not the other way around.

This is the vision to which all Semioticians aspire, and it is a scientific vision. It is not scientific as the positivist would wish, as an *offshoot* of the natural sciences; but it is scientific as a *parallel* to the natural sciences. The Semioticians themselves point out analogies between the past development of the natural sciences and their own planned development of the human sciences.

In the first place, there is an analogy between the way in which Copernicus and Galileo displaced man from the natural world and the way in which the Semioticians hope to displace man from the cultural world. According to the Semioticians, the revolutions that founded modern science were above all revolutions against anthropocentrism and anthropomorphism. Copernicus, for instance, overcame the Ptolemaic anthropocentrism that put human experience automatically in the centre of things. Copernicus looked at the universe impersonally and mathematically, rather than from man's own position out-

wards. Galileo likewise defeated the Aristotelian anthropomorphism that attributed to moving objects a kind of inward,
subjectively centred volition – so that a rolling ball slowed down
because it no longer wanted to go on. Galileo took the inwardness out of objects, and explained their motion by friction and
momentum – two forces which can be neither perceived through
the senses nor felt through empathetic imagination, but which
must be deduced impersonally and mathematically, quite outside of experience. By analogy, the Semioticians hope to take the
inwardness out of human individuals, and explain human
culture by forces of social meaning – forces which can neither be
perceived (behaviouristically) through the senses nor felt
through empathetic imagination, but which must be deduced
impersonally and (even) mathematically, quite outside of
experience.

Such impersonal and mathematical deductions are validated
over direct experience mainly by the principle of superior
simplicity. Thus the hypothesis of a rotating sun-circling earth
was able to replace the enormous number of separate cycles
needed to calculate the movement of the moon, the stars and
each individual planet in the Ptolemaic system. And thus the
hypothesis of friction and momentum was able to introduce
calculation for the first time into an area of study that Aristotle
had left in a state of mere incalculable multiplicity. For whereas
Aristotle's individualized volitions made every moving object a
separate case, Galileo's two forces were the same for all cases,
differing only in the proportions of their combination. By
analogy, the Semioticians propose to consider human beings as
differing combinations of the same forces of social meaning, and
thereby hope to introduce calculation into an area of study
which remains incalculable as long as every human being is
treated as a separate individualized case. The Semioticians'
goal is the ultimate goal of all science: to explain the multiplicity
of appearances from a smaller number of underlying realities.

There is another and more recent analogy with the natural
sciences that Semioticians can claim. For the natural sciences in
the twentieth century have shifted away from the solidity of
nineteenth-century materialism: now it is the concept of the
force-field that predominates. This is most notably true in
atomic physics, of course, where the atom is no longer a cluster

of solid particles but a pattern of insubstantial 'wavicles'. De Broglie, who broached the new view in 1924, envisaged electrons as mere points of intersection in systems of wave-energy. When French Semioticians think favourably of the natural sciences in the twentieth century, they think perhaps especially of the revolution wrought by this French physicist.

Unlike atomic physics, though, Semiotics is still more of a scientific aspiration than a realized science. Neither modern western society nor any other society has yet been satisfactorily explained as a single cultural force-field. As yet, there are only fragmentary explanations in separated disciplines of sign-study. But the Semioticians are confident of a forthcoming grand convergence. They are confident of finding the ultimate forces of social meaning that weave through every kind of cultural code: from codes of style (car-styles, furniture-styles, fashion in clothes, etc.) to codes of visual imagery (advertisement photographs, films, etc.); from codes of behaviour (ritual, etiquette, body language, etc.) to codes of ideology (religions, moral institutions, family structures, etc.); and from codes of narrative (myths, comic strips, TV shows, etc.) to the code of the Unconscious. In the prophetic words of Barthes:

> The form of the signified in the garment system is probably partly the same as that of the signified in the food system, being, as they are, both articulated on the large-scale opposition of work and festivity, activity and leisure. One must therefore foresee a total ideological description, common to all the systems of a given synchrony.[12]

The Semioticians foresee a future unification of the human sciences, analogous, once again, to the unification already achieved between astronomy, physics and chemistry in the natural sciences.

However, we shall not here examine the progress (or otherwise) of the Semioticians towards their goal. For Superstructuralism has since changed its orientation and objectives, and the scientific aspiration now appears as something of a dead end in relation to the movement as a whole. In fact, the movement as a whole does not imitate the usual trajectory of the natural sciences: that is, there is no settling down to the hard work of filling in the details once the general framework has been established. On the contrary, it is the general framework itself which has continued to develop and provide further fuel for the progress of the movement. Superstructuralism has ascended in a philosophical direction, leaving behind its original roots in the human sciences.

Part Two

Superstructuralism becomes philosophical

Preliminaries

The insights described in Part One amount to a Superstructuralist way of thinking, but not, as yet, a Superstructuralist philosophy. For although we may be forced to admit that the effects of Culture and Society run much deeper than we ever imagined, we can still choose to view such effects as illusions or impositions, to be measured against some more fundamental reality. The language category of 'rape', for instance, would still be an illusion in relation to what-really-happened; and the 'glamour' of wine would still be an imposition in relation to our real tastes and preferences. Being true to the world and being true to ourselves might have turned out to be much rarer conditions than we used to think – yet that would only make them all the more valuable. The insights of Superstructuralism, as so far described, are not incompatible with a philosophical belief in the ultimate reality of objective things or subjective ideas.

The philosophy of Existentialism exemplifies just such a situation. For, in their vision of how ordinary people ordinarily live their lives, the Existentialists also give enormous weight to the power of received social signs. Considerable portions of Heidegger's *Being and Time* and Sartre's *Being and Nothingness* are devoted to showing how easily human beings slip into making institutions of themselves, how frequently they are governed by external roles and images, and, above all, how deeply they fall under the spell of language. In his autobiographical essay *Words*, Sartre even goes so far as to explain his whole childhood and adolescent personality as the product of other people's words. For Sartre and Heidegger, received social signs run so deep that we can break free from them only by going through the experience of the Absurd – only by confronting an utterly blank world denuded of all ordinary socially created intelligibility, only by discovering an utterly bare self denuded of all ordinary socially created personality. An extraordinary and desperate kind of experience: yet Sartre and Heidegger give us the moral obligation of going through it. For the mere possibility of the experience enables the Existentialist philosopher to turn the tables on his own vision of how ordinary people ordinarily live their lives.

But when the Superstructuralists develop the philosophical implications of *their* vision, they refuse to allow any such escape-clause. According to the Superstructuralists, we cannot live as human beings below the level of language categories and social meanings because it is language categories and social meanings that make us human in the first place. Thus Althusser argues that a child is only a 'small animal' until language categories have been acquired, and will never be anything more than a 'wolf-child' if they are not acquired.[1] There is no deeper subjective reality underlying the ordinary socially created self, and no deeper objective reality underlying the ordinary socially created intelligibility of the world.

This turns our usual picture of the universe quite upside down. For language categories and social meanings are now the ultimate reality, coming before objective things and subjective ideas. We are looking at a more absolute and generalized manifestation of the two kinds of inversion considered in Part One. In effect, the priority of Culture over Nature now appears as a priority of the Sign over Objective Things, and the priority of Society over the Individual now appears as a priority of the Sign over Subjective Ideas. Needless to say, such a demotion of objective things is particularly disturbing to anyone who shares the traditional Anglo-Saxon respect for the concrete physical world.

This new picture of the universe is also a new picture of the sign itself. When language categories and social meanings are given a primary and self-sufficient status, we can no longer reduce them to a multitude of individual events inside a multitude of individual skulls. They are no longer *subjective* – because they come before us and exist outside of us. In this respect, their existence resembles the existence that we commonly attribute to objective things – and yet they are also obviously not *things*. In order to give a primary and self-sufficient status to language categories and social meanings, we must manage to think of a kind of objectivity which is not the objectivity of things, and of a kind of idea which is not the idea of a subjective mind. No longer can we speak of mere false 'reification' and 'hypostasis' whenever we see ideas taking on a 'thing-ish' objectivity.

In fact, the usual notion of truth and falsity becomes essentially irrelevant in this new picture. For when objective things and subjective ideas lose *their* primary and self-sufficient status, there can be no fundamental role for truth as a correspondence between the realm of subjective ideas and the realm of objective things. And when language categories and social meanings achieve the status of objective ideas, they effectively straddle the two realms and can no longer be evaluated relative to anything else. They become simply necessary and inescapable. And this, once again, is particularly disturbing to anyone who shares the traditional Anglo-Saxon respect for 'the Truth'.

In Part Two, then, I shall be looking at the priority of the Sign over Objective Things and Subjective Ideas, especially in so far as such priority tends to demote the concrete physical world and the usual notion of truth. I shall be following through further developments in the key Superstructuralist field of language theory, and I shall be examining the theories of scientific knowledge advanced by Althusser and Foucault. It is in this latter field that the concrete physical world and the usual notion of truth suffer their greatest demotion. But first I shall make a detour into the past, and attempt to show how the philosophical position of Superstructuralism relates to other, earlier philosophies.

6
Metaphysical philosophy

(i)

To the extent that the philosophical position of Superstructuralism turns upon an attribution of *objectivity* to *ideas*, it is by no means so novel a position as the Superstructuralists themselves imagine. Objective Idealism, the philosophy of Hegel, turns upon exactly the same attribution. And Hegel himself stands in line of descent from Spinoza and Plato. This is the European tradition of Metaphysical philosophy.

This tradition has seldom been understood, let alone favoured, in Anglo-Saxon countries. From the viewpoint of Anglo-Saxon empiricism, it has seemed quite sufficient to attend to the 'I'-philosophy tradition of Descartes, Kant and Husserl; and this other European tradition has been taken as merely a madder and more mystical development of the same thing. But to understand Metaphysical philosophy, we need to understand the logic of a position as different from 'I'-philosophy as 'I'-philosophy is itself different from empiricism. To understand Metaphysical philosophy (albeit with a great deal of simplification), we need to map out the differences between all three positions.

The empiricist position, to begin with, is oriented towards 'natural' objective things, untouched by human hand or mind. For empiricists, the human mind comes properly in second place; if it comes first, it can only impose distorting presuppositions and artificial prejudices upon the outside world. Hence the empiricists' goal of stripping experience back to an immediate state of particular, concrete, passively received sense-data. Under the concept of what's 'natural', this state is the most uninterpreted, most outward-facing, and therefore most sure and certain state possible. This is the primary and self-sufficient base upon which knowledge is to be founded.

The Metaphysical argument against empiricism is proposed by Plato, repeated by Spinoza, and directed specifically against the Anglo-Saxons by Hegel. It is an argument that, long before the language philosophies of the twentieth century, already effectively equates human thinking with human language. On this argument, we *know* that we are experiencing sense-data only in so far as we think the experience in verbal units. We *know* darkness or warmth only in so far as we think 'dark' or 'warm', and we think 'dark' or 'warm' only in so far as we make general distinctions of 'dark' as against 'light' or 'warm' as against 'cold'. By the time we can become acquainted with our own experience, it has always already been filtered through a system of ideas and found significant. Unless or until it is found significant, it is no more than stimulation on the retina or in the nerve-endings of the skin; and we can never actually live at the level of what happens on the retina or in the nerve-endings of our skin. Yet this is precisely what empiricist philosophers seek to do, when they seek to capture experience in a purely uninterpreted and outward-facing state. In reality, of course, they only construct this state *retrospectively*, as a matter of theoretical necessity.

Descartes, Kant and Husserl also argue against empiricism. They too insist that we never *know* uninterpreted sense-data; by the time we can become acquainted with our own experience, it has always already been filtered through a system of innate ideas, or of *a priori* categories, or of projective horizons. But these systems reside inside the minds of individual subjects, who create the world outwardly from the centre of their individual selves. The 'I'-philosophers advance subjective ideas into first place ahead of objective things. Hence the goal of stripping experience back to the self-conscious inward-facing core of the *cogito* or the transcendental ego. For the 'I'-philosophers, the most sure and certain state of experience is the state that lies 'closest in'. This is the primary and self-sufficient base upon which knowledge is to be founded – primary and self-sufficient not in the way of objective things, but in the way of an undetermined creative source. Not surprisingly, Descartes, Kant and Husserl all make a space for individual free will in their philosophies.

For Metaphysical philosophers, on the other hand, what lies 'closest in' is no more sure and certain than what's 'natural'. *Their* systems of ideas do not reside inside the minds of individual subjects. In Plato's philosophy, the Forms are fixed in a timeless realm outside the universe; in Spinoza's philosophy, the Modes and Attributes of God are immanent in every part of the universe, human or non-human; and in Hegel's philosophy, the Categories are instituted in human *society*, over and above any individual subject. Such systems of ideas are not thought *by* or *from* our minds; rather, they 'think themselves', only passing *through* or *into* our minds. The Metaphysical philosophers advance objective ideas into first place, ahead of both objective things and subjective ideas.

The opposition to subjective ideas as a base for knowledge appears in Spinoza as an explicit opposition to Descartes, and in Hegel as an explicit opposition to Kant. Spinoza rejects the famous Cartesian notion of subjectivity, that spiralling inwardness which hives ideas off into the exclusive privacy of the *cogito*, away from the world. He thereby overcomes the famous Cartesian problem of dualism, that lack of connection between things out in the world and the ideas of those things in the human mind. In Spinoza's philosophy, the ideas of things *are* the things; and such ideas-or-things are just as much out in the world as the things themselves ever were. What's more, the human mind is also the idea of a thing – the idea of a particular human body. And such a mind-or-body is just as much on a level with the rest of the world as the body itself ever was. So much for our unique creative individualities and transcendental ego-centricities. In Spinoza's philosophy, we are ruled by exactly the same determinism as rules the world at large. Indeed, Spinoza reduces the human experience of desire and moral obligation to purely quantitative flows of energy in a way that oddly anticipates Freud. But Spinoza's rejection of free will is not the same as the natural scientists' rejection of free will, and does not lead to a purely physical view of the world. Spinoza attacks the *subjectivity* of ideas, but he does not embrace the objectivity of *things*.

Hegel, for his part, opposes Kant's famous morality of the individual conscience. For Hegel, the morality of the individual conscience belongs only to a particular phase of society, a particular phase of legalism and individual rights. (Like Althusser, he seems here to be thinking especially of the classically bourgeois seventeenth and eighteenth centuries.) For Hegel, such 'Civil Society' is essentially unbalanced and alienating, and must eventually give way to 'the State'. 'The State' is the complete and final form of society, when individual interests are absorbed into and identified with the interests of the social collectivity as a whole. And this is really no more than the actualization of the situation that has existed all along. For, in Hegel's Objective Idealism, the notion of the individual self never arises directly out of personal experience anyway; one recognizes an individual self in oneself only in so far as it is first recognized there by others. (This reading of section IVA of the *Phenomenology* pursues Hegel's insights in quite the opposite direction to Sartre's Existentialist reading of the same section.) The individual self is never truly primary or self-sufficient; it is always socially created before it is creative, always socially determined before it is free. The English Hegelian, F. H. Bradley, expresses it all with admirable lucidity:

> The child . . . is born . . . into a living world. . . . He does not even think of his separate self; he grows with his world, his mind fills and orders itself; and when he can separate himself from that world, and know himself apart from it, then by that time his self, the object of his self-consciousness, is penetrated, infected, characterized by the existence of others. Its content implies in every fibre relations of community. He learns, or already perhaps has learnt, to speak, and here he appropriates the common heritage of his race, the tongue that he makes his own is his country's language, it is . . . the same that others speak, and it carries into his mind the ideas and sentiments of the race . . . and stamps them in indelibly. He grows up in an atmosphere of example and general

custom. .... The soul within him is saturated, is filled, is
qualified by, it has assimilated, has got its substance,
has built itself up from, it *is* one and the same life with the
universal life.[1]

The closeness of the relation between Objective Idealism and
Superstructuralism could hardly be made more plain.

(ii)

None the less, there are still some differences to reckon with.
One is purely terminological, and arises from the rather special
way in which Superstructuralists understand the term 'Idealism'. For 'Idealism' is very much a dirty word in their vocabulary, and they often give the impression of being violently
opposed to Idealism in every conceivable form. But in fact they
are violently opposed only to the Subjective form of Idealism.
Subjective Idealism reduces the universe to mere subjective
mental contents, and tends to get itself trapped inside the
separate individual skull, unable to reach out from the subjective to the objective world. Such was the nemesis of the later
Husserl. But the objective ideas of Hegel and Spinoza and Plato
straddle both worlds from the beginning. Terminological
appearances notwithstanding, Objective Idealism and Subjective Idealism are quite unrelated philosophical positions.

In fact, the objective ideas of the Metaphysical philosophers
are ideas only in a rather special sense. They are ideas not as
mental contents in general are ideas, but specifically as abstractions are ideas. Images and perceptual data and all such mental
'solids' are excluded; the universe of objective ideas is a universe
of empty categories and relational forms. The Metaphysical
philosophers are also Abstractionists – and the same can be said
for the Superstructuralists.

However, it must be admitted that Plato, Spinoza and Hegel
do tend to lapse into an older and less rigorously abstract way of
conceiving objective ideas. They tend to interpret objective
ideas in terms of a religious concept of God or Spirit. Of all
philosophical traditions, the Metaphysical tradition has always
been the most spiritually oriented. For the concept of God or
Spirit is precisely the concept of a mind outside of any individual

subjective mind. But this concept is still formed upon an analogy with the individual subjective mind; there remains always a kind of inwardness about the thinking of a Divine Mind. Even when God is totally depersonalized, even geometricized, in Spinoza's philosophy, He still stands (as *natura naturans*) always a little behind the universe (as *natura naturata*), expressing Himself through it from the inside outwardly. Similarly with Hegel's equally depersonalized concept of *Geist*. Even though Hegel objectifies his Categories in the laws and customs and institutions of society, he still feels it necessary to give them the support of a more inward Spirit of Society, a hidden force and source underlying external social manifestations. It is this *Geist*-ly side of Hegel that Althusser most objects to, quite justifiably from the Superstructuralist point of view.[2]

The Superstructuralists shed the religious baggage. They are able to do so because they have a way of objectifying abstractions that leaves behind even the analogy with the individual subjective mind: they objectify abstractions in the form of signs and language categories. And signs and language categories are communicated *between* individual human minds rather than lying *behind* them. With the concept of signs and language categories, it becomes much easier to think of abstractions as simple external manifestations, simply on a level with everything else in the universe. It becomes much easier to think of them as existing all by themselves, neither within human minds nor within some special superhuman mind. Superstructuralism thus represents a kind of natural next step for Metaphysical philosophy. In a sense, Metaphysical philosophy always needed to become a philosophy of language; indeed, we have already seen a philosophy of language peeping out in the argument against empiricism and in Bradley's description of the growing child. More particularly, Superstructuralism represents a kind of natural next step in the progression that runs from Plato's Forms (fixed in a realm outside the universe) to Spinoza's Modes and Attributes (immanent everywhere within the universe) to Hegel's Categories (instituted specifically in human society). The concept of signs and language categories brings Hegel's general notion of social institution down to an even more practical and determinate mode of existence.

By finally shedding the religious baggage, Superstructuralism also enables us to see more clearly the essential logic of the Metaphysical position. For the Superstructuralists do not merely oppose the empiricist philosophy of objective things and the 'I'-philosophy of subjective ideas – they oppose the relation between empiricist philosophy and 'I'-philosophy together. From the viewpoint of Superstructuralist philosophy, these two other philosophies are but the two halves of a single error. Certainly, the empiricists battle for the supremacy of objective things over subjective ideas, and the 'I'-philosophers battle for the supremacy of subjective ideas over objective things: yet both sides agree that things are indeed objective and ideas are indeed subjective. Both sides work to equate the notion of ideas with a notion of inwardness, and a notion of the outside world with the notion of things. It is a classic case of a polarization which, under an appearance of conflict, actually defines a single conceptual dimension to the exclusion of all other possibilities.

We can give a name to this conceptual dimension: it is the dimension of 'experience'. For experience as we commonly conceive it is precisely the place where objective things make contact with subjective ideas. Superstructuralist philosophy thus proposes to outleap the dimension of experience, to start from a starting point outside of experience. And such a move in philosophy is precisely the move that has always been described – and often despised – as 'metaphysical'. But with the modern example of Superstructuralism before us, we can no longer dismiss Metaphysical philosophy quite as easily as Anglo-Saxon philosophers are wont to dismiss it. We can no longer regard it as the product of mere muddled dreaming and religious mystification. Metaphysical philosophy is undoubtedly paradoxical, undoubtedly beyond all ordinary common sense: but there is a very real logic to it none the less.

7

More Structural Linguistics

(i)

The relation between Superstructuralism and Metaphysical philosophy is already apparent in Saussure's concept of 'langue'. For the concept of 'langue' is precisely the concept of an objective idea. Before Saussure, language was traditionally viewed in terms of a physical sound on the one hand, and a mental idea on the other: the former existing in the world of objective things, and the latter inside individual subjective minds. But Saussure's signifier, in so far as it is taken up into 'langue', is not a thing but, as we have seen, a category of sound, a conceptualized 'sound-image'.[1] And Saussure's signified, in so far as it is taken up into 'langue', is not an event inside individual subjective minds but, as we have seen, an ever-present, pre-existing social reality. In the realm of 'langue', the traditional dualism between objective things and subjective ideas simply falls away.

Saussure does not consistently abide by the logic of his own concept of 'langue', however. He is always liable to lapse back into mentalistic inside-the-skull interpretations. It is a later linguist, Emile Benveniste, who pursues the concept of 'langue' through to its more rigorous conclusions. With Benveniste's re-reading of Saussure, the Superstructuralist revolution in linguistics is decisively shorn of all old psychologistic trappings.

For Benveniste, even Saussure's way of distinguishing between signifier and signified is a hangover from the past. Against this side of Saussure, Benveniste sets a rather different side, which appears in the assertion that 'it is from the interdependent whole [of the sign] that one must start'.[2] Benveniste pays especial attention to the remarkably suggestive Chapter IV in Part Two of the *Course in General Linguistics*, where Saussure claims that thought and sound are mere unknowable shapeless masses in themselves, which divide out into units only when they come together and react upon each other. From this it follows that, so far as we can *know* at all, the relation between sound and thought always precedes any particular units of sound or any particular units of thought. Hence the real practical difficulty of ever thinking a word's signified apart from its signifier, or its signifier apart from its signified. As Benveniste says: 'Together [signifieds and signifiers] are imprinted on my mind, together they evoke each other under any circumstance.'[3] The fact that the relation between sound and thought is conventional does not make it any the less inescapable. On the contrary, this is exactly the kind of convention that we cannot delve down under or check out for ourselves.

So, whereas Saussure speaks of the arbitrariness of the convention that unites a given signifier to a given signified, Benveniste changes the emphasis and speaks of its necessity. Saussure's way of speaking, according to Benveniste, allows the signified to separate out from the sign, and encourages Saussure to present it as a kind of independent mental image – as when he embodies the signified of the word 'tree' in a picture of a tree. Such a notion of mental imagery is quite contrary to Saussure's own express claims that signifieds are concepts 'defined not by their positive content', and that the combination of sound and thought '*produces a form, not a substance*'.[4] If a picture of a tree can do the same work as the signified of the word 'tree', then the whole vaunted interdependence of thought and language disintegrates.

For Benveniste, Saussure's notion of mental imagery indicates the insidious return of the referent. Although Saussure allows no explicit role to the referent, he fails to think of the signified entirely apart from it. 'In reality, Saussure was always thinking of the representation of the *real object* (although he spoke of the "idea").[5] Saussure falls under the influence of the traditional assumption that signifieds are naturally and immediately related to the things of the outside world – just as a picture is naturally and immediately related to the thing it pictures.

Of course, as soon as the referent returns, a genuine arbitrariness *is* involved. For the physical sound 't-r-ee' certainly bears no relation to real trees in the outside world: 'What is arbitrary is that one certain sign and no other is applied to a certain element of reality, and not to any other.'[6] The issue, though, is as to whether this arbitrariness falls between signifier and signified or between signified and referent. Under Saussure's assumption of a natural and immediate relation between signified and referent, the signified moves over to the side of objective things and leaves the signifier isolated and cut off. But Saussure also thinks of signifieds as formal values in a differential system, constituted not in relation to objective things but in relation to one another, by exactly the same process as that which constitutes signifiers. By focusing upon signifieds as formal values, Benveniste turns the tables completely: the signified now moves over to the side of the signifier, and it is the world of objective things that is left isolated and cut off.

This, when one looks at it, is an extraordinary conclusion. It is all very well to reject the excessive importance that reference assumed for the Logical Atomists and the Logical Positivists, but it is something else again to make language so hermetic that meaning gets separated from objective things altogether. Yet this is the kind of conclusion to which the logic of Metaphysical philosophy has always led. When ideas are outside *first*, they inevitably tend to overwhelm the other outside of things. Thus Plato's Forms become so powerful an explanation for phenomenal appearances that the ordinary solid world only survives as amorphous, shapeless Matter; and Hegel's Categories become so powerful an explanation for phenomenal appearances that, especially in the Hegelian Philosophy of Nature, the ordinary solid world has no existence apart from them at all. Objective ideas, once summoned up, have a way of rendering everything else unspeakable, unthinkable, unknowable, and ultimately irrelevant. Needless to say, such absolutism calls for opposition; and I shall be suggesting an obvious objection or two at the end of this chapter. But first it will be useful to see how linguists after Saussure developed the crucial notion of formal value in a differential system.

(ii)

Saussure's version of differentiation is not in itself sufficient to constitute signs entirely in relation to one another and without relation to objective things. In Saussure's version, 'all words used to express related ideas limit each other reciprocally', just as neighbouring holes in a net limit one another reciprocally.[7] But the notion of neighbourhood, straightforward enough in the case of the net, becomes highly problematical in the case of language. Neighbourhood between words is not merely a matter of side-by-side contiguity, but a matter of something shared. So, although the meaning of the word 'rape' sets itself against the meaning of the word 'love', it none the less covers the same kind of territory – as the meaning of the word 'poodle' does not. Similarly and even more obviously in Saussure's own example of a mutual differentiation between the meanings of the words 'redouter', 'craindre' and 'avoir peur' (very roughly, 'to dread', 'to fear' and 'to be afraid'): although these meanings limit one another in their finer implications, they have almost everything else in common. In the case of language, it becomes impossible to think of differentiation in terms of such simple absolute boundaries as separate the holes in a net.

Saussure fails to recognize this impossiblity because he has his own psychologistic way of deriving the neighbours for a word. In effect, he presents a particular word to the mind, and allows it to call up other words by free mental association:

> [Words] that have something in common are associated in the memory, resulting in groups marked by diverse relations. For instance, the French word *enseignement* 'teaching' will unconsciously call to mind a host of other words (*enseigner* 'teach', *renseigner* 'acquaint', etc.; or *armament* 'armament', *changement* 'amendment' etc.; or *éducation* 'education', *apprentissage* 'apprenticeship' etc.)[8]

One word leads on to the memory of another, in whatever sequence may happen to flow from the individual mind.

Clearly, this has nothing to do with the realm where differentiation operates, the realm of 'langue'. In 'langue', a word does not *lead on* to its neighbours, but rather, by its very existence, *presupposes* them. And such presupposition does not take place in any individual mind; indeed it does not *take place* as a mental event at all. By leaving what words have in common on a merely psychological level, Saussure disables the principle of differentiation and makes it impossible to think 'langue' systematically.

The attempt to think 'langue' systematically compelled later linguists to a new version of differentiation. The crucial advance was first made by Roman Jakobson in the somewhat specialized field of phonology, dealing not with words as the minimal units of meaning but with phonemes as the minimal units of sound. What's new in Jakobson's model is the admission of 'the possibility of pronouncing two elements simultaneously', which Saussure denied.[9] Saussurean differentiation between phonemes, like Saussurean differentiation between word-meaning, was all-on-a-plane, spread flat like a net. But Jakobson unfolds out of the phoneme a simultaneous multiplicity of 'distinctive features', abstracts out of the simple immediate sound a complexity of ulterior levels. A 'p' or a 'k' or a 't' is no longer like a single musical note but like a chord.[10]

The justification for this abstraction – as for all abstraction – is the gain in rigour and clarity that it makes possible. When phonemes are thus unfolded, the relation between phonemes can be explained as a matter of sharing on some levels and differing on others. Instead of a simple absolute boundary between the sound of a 'p' and the sound of a 'k', we can recognize that a 'p' and a 'k' are similar to the extent that both are 'grave' (that is, peripherally constricted in the mouth), but different to the extent that a 'p' is 'diffuse' (backwardly flanged in the mouth) whereas a 'k' is 'compact' (forwardly flanged in the mouth). Or we can recognize that a 'p' and a 't' are similar to the extent that both are 'diffuse', but different to the extent that a 'p' is 'grave' whereas a 't' is 'acute' (that is, centrally constricted in the mouth). By unfolding just twelve essential levels of sharing or differing, Jakobson claims to be able to describe all possible phonemes in all possible languages.

On those levels where phonemes *differ*, there is also a new rigour and clarity about the differing. A whole phoneme differs in *some* respect from every other whole phoneme in the phonetic alphabet. But the division into levels divides the number of alternatives that need to be considered on any particular level. When the 'flanged' aspect of sound is abstracted out from the whole sound of a 'p', for instance, it turns out that there are only a very few ways in which sound can be flanged. In fact, according to Jakobson, sound can only be flanged either backwardly for 'diffuse' or forwardly for 'compact'. Similarly on all of Jakobson's twelve levels. There is only either 'grave' (peripheral constriction) or 'acute' (central constriction); only either 'nasal' (introduction of the nasal resonator) or 'oral' (exclusion of the nasal resonator); only either 'consonantal' (obstruction in the vocal tract) or 'non-consonantal' (no obstruction in the vocal tract); and so on. On every level, Jakobson manages to find a difference between just two alternatives.

A difference between just two alternatives is a very special kind of difference: a contrast or binary opposition. A whole phoneme can be set against no single specific counterbalancing phoneme; as Jakobson says, 'the phoneme *b* does not call univocally, reversibly, and necessarily for a definite opposite'.[11] In Saussure's version of differentiation, one phoneme has to be cut out against a much larger surround of all the other phonemes; there is no quantitative balance, and it is hard to believe that there is any qualitative balance either. That is, it is hard to believe that our specific conception of a 'p' involves an *equally specific* conception of each and every other phoneme against which the 'p' must define itself. (And indeed, would not the 'p' ultimately have to define itself against non-phonetic sounds too? Against the sound of a sneeze and the sound of a motorbike?) It seems more natural to view the 'p' as a determinate 'figure' set off against the indeterminate 'ground' of all that is *not*-'p'. But this is the *Gestalt* version of differentiation – which requires original creative activity on the part of the subject, and goes hand in hand with Husserlian 'I'-philosophy. For it is an effort of free consciousness which makes the 'figure' come forward and the 'ground' retreat. Needless to say, this is not the direction that Saussure intended his linguistics to take.

Jakobson's binary oppositions allow Structural Linguistics to take the direction Saussure intended. In a binary opposition between distinctive features, the 'diffuse' sound of a 'p' can be set against the single specific counterbalancing alternative of 'compact' sound. On its own particular level, this opposition covers all possibilities: whatever is not 'compact' is 'diffuse' and whatever is not 'diffuse' is 'compact'. We are no longer looking at a bounded 'figure' on an unbounded 'ground', but at two similarly bounded and unbounded moieties on either side of a universe-wide dividing line. Only thus can mutual definition become truly reciprocal, only thus can our conception of what 'diffuse' *is* involve an *equally specific* conception of the 'compact' that it *is not*. As Jakobson puts it:

> The oppositions of the distinctive features are real, logical, binary oppositions, and the one element of each of these oppositions necessarily includes the opposing element. Breadth can not be thought without narrowness, back formation can not be thought without front formation, roundedness can not be thought without unroundedness, etc.[12]

The two terms of a binary opposition logically imply and presuppose one another on every occasion.

The rigour and clarity of Jakobson's system also extends to a hierarchical ordering of the twelve levels. According to Jakobson, some oppositions are earlier and more fundamental than others. Thus the level on which 'p' differs from 't' is more fundamental than the level on which 'r' differs from 'l' – which is why many languages (for example, Japanese) fail to distinguish between 'r' and 'l', but almost no languages fail to distinguish between 'p' and 't'. This hierarchical ordering also determines the order in which a child acquires phonetic distinctions. The opposition between alveolar and velar stops arrives later than the opposition between labial and alveolar stops, for example: all children go through a phase of pronouncing 'cat' something like 'tat'. Conversely, in aphasia and language loss the opposition between alveolar and velar stops disappears more easily than the opposition between alveolar and labial stops.[13]

This order of acquisition can be traced back to the very birth of language in the child. The oppositions on which all others are founded turn out to be precisely those oppositions which make possible the child's earliest words – 'mama' and 'papa'. Jakobson describes the 'p'–'a' combination as follows:

From the articulatory point of view the two constituents of this utterance represent polar configurations of the vocal tract: in /p/ the tract is closed at its very end while in /a/ it is opened as widely as possible at the front and narrowed toward the back, thus assuming the horn-shape of a megaphone. This combination of two extremes is also apparent on the acoustic level: the labial stop presents a momentary burst of sound without any great concentration of energy in a particular frequency band, whereas in the vowel /a/ there is no strict limitation of time, and the energy is concentrated in a relatively narrow region of maximum aural sensitivity. . . . Consequently, the diffuse stop with its maximal reduction in the energy output offers the closest approach to silence, while the open vowel represents the highest energy output of which the human vocal apparatus is capable.[14]

The word 'papa' depends upon the earliest dividing line that can be drawn across a previously shapeless mass of pre-phonetic sound.

So, right from the very start, phonetic units are never experienced independently, but only in pairs, falling away simultaneously on either side of a single dividing line. 'In a child's mind the pair is anterior to isolated objects', says Jakobson, referring especially to the psychological theory of H. Wallon.[15] As Saussure also claimed, differentiation precedes the units differentiated. But Saussure himself could never carry this principle back to the birth of language in the child. Indeed, he could never explain the actual acquisition of 'langue' at all. For Saussure was not dealing with distinctive features in pairs, but with phonemes in multitudes. And if every phoneme exists only by virtue of what it is not, and what it is not is every other phoneme, then there can be no way of making a start from any particular dividing line between any particular phonemes. The system of phonetic differentiation would have to be acquired all at once, in its entirety. But so sudden a leap from nothing to everything is virtually unthinkable – and Saussure did not try to think it. Instead, he sliced 'langue' out from the full reality of language with a special methodological restriction. Saussurean 'langue' can be viewed only synchronically, only as it already completely exists at a given moment.

With Jackobson's version of differentiation, 'langue' overcomes this restriction and conquers the dimension of time. Now
there is a bridge between nothing and everything, between the
shapeless mass of pre-phonetic sound and the detailed complexity of a complete phonetic system. Now it becomes possible to
constitute 'langue' through successive levels of differentiation,
with only a simple single dividing line to be thought on any one
level. No longer is linguistic explanation merely like describing
the rules of chess as they already completely exist; now it is like
actually bringing them into existence. (Consider, for instance,
how the rules for moving individual chess-pieces might be
brought into existence by successive binary differentiations of
the total possibilities for movement on the board: *single-step*
movement in any direction as for the King versus *unlimited*
movement in any direction as for the Queen; movement in *any*
direction as for the King and Queen versus movement in a *single*
direction as for the Bishops and Rooks; movement in a *diagonal*
direction as for the Bishop versus movement in a *lateral* direction
as for the Rook; and so on.) Jakobson's version of differentiation
gives 'langue' new claims upon the full reality of language, and
thereby upon the full reality of the world in general. And since,
as we have seen, the concept of 'langue' is the concept of an
objective idea, these new claims indicate an increasingly close
approach to Metaphysical philosophy.

In fact, there has always been an affinity between binarism
and Metaphysical philosophy. Just as any philosophy which
seeks to found the world upon objects before relations must
inevitably incline towards objects in their most elementary
atomic form, so any philosophy which seeks to found the world
upon relations before objects must inevitably incline towards
relations in their most elementary binary form. Binary thinking
thus appears in the philosophy of Plato, especially in the *Sophist*,
where Being divides into Identity versus Difference, Motion
versus Rest, and so on. Similarly in the philosophy of Spinoza,
where Substance divides into Extension versus Thought, Extension divides into Motion versus Rest, and so on. And binary
thinking becomes quite obsessive in the philosophy of Hegel,
where the Categories think themselves into existence through a
dialectic of Being versus Nothing, the One versus the Many,
Repulsion versus Attraction, and so on. Of course, Jakobson

is no follower of Hegel or Spinoza or Plato; indeed, he is much more of a scientist and much less of a philosopher than Saussure. But he is caught up in the logic of 'langue' none the less.

(iii)

There are doubts amongst linguists as to the validity of Jakobson's phonetics. After all, there is no reason to suppose that our speech organs are physically constituted in binary formations. If Jakobson is to be believed, the way we *think* sound must take total precedence over more mundane considerations of vocal anatomy. However, I shall leave this debate to the specialists in the field. The issues become larger and more controversial when linguists attempt to carry the same binarist model over into semantics.

It must be admitted that no systematization of semantics has yet come close to the rigour and clarity of Jakobson's systematization of phonetics. Hjelmslev, Greimas, Prieto, Eco and others have worked out the theory for a comprehensive semantics along Jakobsonian lines, but they have demonstrated the practice in only a few especially easy and appropriate cases. In Structuralist semantics, the aspiration far outruns the realization – but it is none the less influential for that.

The first major attempt to systematize semantics was made by Louis Hjelmslev.[16] In Hjelmslev's 'glossematics', the single word-meaning is unfolded out into a simultaneous multiplicity of semantic elements. Differentiation between word-meanings is no longer a matter of simple absolute boundaries, but a matter of sharing on some levels and differing on others. Thus we can recognize that the meaning of 'mare' is similar to the meaning of 'stallion' to the extent that both are equine, but different to the extent that 'mare' is female whereas 'stallion' is male. Or we can recognize that the meaning of 'mare' is similar to the meaning of 'ewe' to the extent that both are female, but different to the extent that 'mare' is equine whereas 'ewe' is ovine. In effect, two dividing lines cut out four word-meanings (mare, stallion, ewe, ram). A sufficiently complex system of dividing lines, so Hjelmslev believed, should make it possible to carry out

Saussure's original programme of describing meaning entirely in terms of differentiation.

Of those who follow in Hjelmslev's footsteps, A. J. Greimas is perhaps the most notable. For Greimas too, the units of verbal meaning (or lexemes) are made up of simultaneous semantic elements (or semes). What's more, Greimas consistently reduces differentiation to pure binary opposition (black versus white, big versus small, etc.), and arranges the levels of opposition hierarchically. 'The lexeme no longer appears to us as a simple collection of semes, but as a composition of semes interconnected by hierarchical relations.'[17] What this means for 'langue' can be seen in Griemas's systematization of the semantics of space:[18]

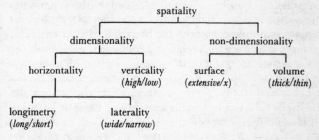

The organization of the semantic lexicon here begins to look rather like the organization of Roget's *Thesaurus*.

This logical order of production also indicates a possible chronological order of production. Theoretically at least, meaning can now be developed all the way from an original shapeless mass of experience to the detailed complexity of a full semantic vocabulary. Theoretically at least, language acquisition can now begin as Lacan suggests in his analysis of the Freudian *fort-da*. In this now-famous case-study, Freud observed his grandson repeatedly hiding and re-finding a cotton reel, whilst uttering 'ŏ' and 'ā' sounds that Freud interpreted as attempts to pronounce the German words 'fort' and 'da' ('here' and 'there'). According to Freud, the cotton reel was the child's symbol for his mother, and the game gave him the illusion of control over her (desirable) presence and (undesirable) absence. Lacan accepts this symbolism, but makes it depend rather less upon the object and rather more upon the words –

which polarize a 'here' and a 'there' location for *both* the mother *and* the cotton reel. According to Lacan, the child's assimilation under the control of language is far more important than the illusion of control over his mother. In effect, the words *as a pair* have drawn a dividing line across a previously shapeless mass of experience. And although the dividing line between a mother's presence or absence may seem a matter of fairly local importance from an adult point of view, from the child's point of view everything in his existence hinges upon it. From the child's point of view, this dividing line spans the universe: a primary differentiation of Presence versus Absence, Positive versus Negative, Being versus Nothing.

We have now reached a convergence between the Jakobsonian version of differentiation and Benveniste's hermetic theory of language. Logically and chronologically, the units of language can now constitute themselves entirely in relation to one another and without relation to outside things. Even the units of meaning no longer conform to any independent natural units; before and apart from language, there is only ever a shapeless mass of experience, a featureless continuum. As Benveniste would claim, the imposition of linguistic dividing lines is essentially arbitrary.

This is a very hard claim to swallow. It looks plausible enough when we are dealing with words like 'here' (versus 'there') or 'long' (versus 'short') or 'hot' (versus 'cold') or 'heavy' (versus 'light'). In such cases, certainly, the dividing line comes from us and not from nature: thus things in themselves show no tendency to be *either* heavy *or* light, rather than anything in between. (In fact, the dividing line between 'heavy' and 'light' has no fixed position, but shifts according to context and the things under consideration.) But it is a different story when we are dealing with words like 'walk' or 'see' or 'cloud' or 'hill'. Can we really believe that nature in *these* cases shows no tendency to make up units of its own, presents no 'lumpishness' for us to erect our words upon?

Of course, there are possible oppositions in these cases too. Thus 'walk' can be polarized against 'run' (as in Roget's *Thesaurus*, where the words appear under opposing heads, 277 and 278). 'Walk' is similar to 'run' to the extent that both describe human locomotion, but different to the extent that 'walk' describes slow motion whereas 'run' describes fast motion. And, as regards the difference, the general dividing line between 'slow' and 'fast' is clearly of the same kind as the dividing line between 'here' and 'there', or 'long' and 'short', or 'hot' and 'cold', or 'light' and 'heavy'. When we look at 'walk' and 'run' in terms of 'slow' and 'fast', it may seem that we are looking at a natural continuum polarized by a purely linguistic dividing line. However, there is much more to the difference between walking and running than a difference in speed. There is first and foremost a difference in action, in the way that the legs stiffen and bend and make contact with the ground. This difference depends upon the empirical fact that the bones and muscles in the legs are arranged in a certain particular structure – and such a structure functions effectively in only *either* a walking *or* a running action. Anything in between would be inefficient if not downright impossible. Human locomotion is not a continuum of possibilities; nature works itself up into some combinations and not others. When we look at 'walk' and 'run' in this light, we see that the different speeds can be derived *as a consequence* of the combinations: a running action provides more forward thrust, while a walking action expends less energy in supporting the weight of the body.

For another example, consider the case of 'hill' as opposed to 'mountain'. Certainly, the two words differ to the extent that 'hill' describes a relatively low landform, whereas 'mountain' describes a relatively high landform; and, certainly, there is no tendency in nature for landforms to be *either* relatively low *or* relatively high, rather than anything in between. But the two words also differ to the extent that 'hill' describes a rounded landform, whereas 'mountain' describes a peaked landform. And here a natural dividing line does come into play – the discontinuity between water and ice. For rounded shapes are typically smoothed out by the gentle erosion of rainwater, and peaked shapes are typically gouged out by the tearing erosion of ice. Since, in any given geographical area, the temperature falls consistently below freezing point at a certain height above sea-level, it follows that landforms which do not attain this height will tend to be rounded at the top, and landforms which exceed this height will tend to be peaked. Once again, nature works itself up into some combinations rather than others – into high-and-peaked or low-and-rounded rather than low-and-peaked or high-and-rounded.

Of course, the natural dividing line between 'hill' and 'mountain' is much more tenuous than that between 'walk' and 'run'. There are innumerable exceptions and in-between cases. But then it would be ridiculous ever to expect absolutely hard-and-fast dividing lines in nature. All we can expect is a degree of 'lumpishness', a bare tendency for certain properties to hang together. Natural dividing lines are relative thinnesses between relative thicknesses – like the grooves in a bar of chocolate. It still takes language to break the bar into completely separate pieces. It still takes language to put the outlines around the units in our minds.

With the aid of the chocolate-bar analogy, we can see why and where and just how much linguistic dividing lines vary from language to language. Structural Linguists, of course, are fond of alluding to such variations as a proof that all linguistic dividing lines are essentially arbitrary. Indeed, they are surprisingly impressed by the fact that any variations whatsoever should exist. But if one expects arbitrariness, then what is impressive is the fact that any equivalences whatsoever should exist. For myself, I remember that, when I first started to learn French (by a somewhat odd system which for a long time taught us to pronounce the words phonetically without teaching us what they meant), I truly expected this new language to divide the world into *entirely* new units; and I was surprised to discover, in the end, that the word 'chien' actually meant something very much like the word 'dog', and the word 'maison' actually meant something very much like the word 'house'!

The chocolate-bar analogy explains the equivalences whilst allowing for the variations. In the first place, the groove allows a degree of variation in the line of the break: no two pieces of chocolate are exactly the same around the edges. Just so, the meaning of the word 'maison' is not exactly the same around the edges as the meaning of the word 'house'. In the second place, not every groove has to be broken: for practical purposes, one often breaks off a chocolate-bar in large chunks, dividing along one groove and ignoring others. Just so, the Eskimos have four separate words for snow where we have only one; just so, the English language recognizes 'mouse' and 'rat' where the Latin language sees only 'mus'. Of course, some of nature's grooves are thinner and more obvious than others; and some become more obvious according to a particular interest or context – according to the particular angle of one's grip on the chocolate-bar, as it were. But, with all the qualifications and complications, it still has to be said that nature is *not* a featureless continuum, and languages do *not* produce dividing lines entirely out of themselves.

The problem for Structural Linguists is that, once they have started explaining language hermetically, they find no reason to stop. There is no *clearly visible* limit where their kind of explanation cuts off. So an original methodological decision to exclude the outside world (explicit in Benveniste and Hjelmslev) gradually turns into a general philosophical principle of unlimited scope.

8
Althusser and science

(i)

While Structural Linguists advance towards a hermetic theory of language, Althusser proposes, even more strangely, a hermetic theory of science. Unlike science as we ordinarily conceive it, Althusser's Science does not stoop to grubbing around for evidence amongst the things of the outside world, but constitutes itself out of virtually nothing but a pure process of thought. This is a Science on the level of Hegel's Science or Spinoza's *scientia intuitiva* – a level from which one looks down upon the limited knowledges that natural scientists produce. This is a Science for philosophers.

But before we explore the connection between Althusser and the Metaphysical philosophers there is one complication to contend with: namely, that while Althusser professes to be a follower of Spinoza, he persistently sets himself against Hegel.[1] In fact, although there are real enough differences between Althusser and Hegel, they are by no means as deep as Althusser wishes to believe them. That Althusser wishes to believe them deep is mainly due to a convoluted bout of theoretical infighting that the French Communist Party was going through in the 1960s. During this period, Althusser was seeking to drive out the influence of Sartre and his Existentialist sympathizers; Sartre had appropriated Hegel for his own subject-oriented purposes and was proclaiming a return to the Hegelian elements in Marx; so Althusser felt obliged to set himself against Hegel. But the Hegel that Althusser sets himself against is the Hegel of Sartre's slewed and selective interpretation. In the 1970s, in his retrospective *Essays in Self-criticism*, Althusser seems to get a clearer picture of the real Hegel, and mellows towards him accordingly.

Althusser also supposes himself to be opposing Hegel when he directs attention towards Marx's later works and away from his earlier works. Sartre had directed attention towards the earlier works because their 'Young Hegelian' attitudes could be made to fit, at a pinch, with Existentialism. But there are Hegelian elements in the later works too – especially in Marx's model for scientific procedure, and especially in the works upon which Althusser draws most heavily (the *1857 Introduction*, the *Grundrisse* and the *Contribution to the Critique of Political Economy*). What could be more Hegelian than the following?

> It would seem to be the proper thing to start with the real and concrete elements, with the actual pre-conditions, *e.g.*, to start in the sphere of economy with population, which forms the basis and the subject of the whole social process of production. Closer consideration shows, however, that this is wrong. Population is an abstraction if, for instance, one disregards the classes of which it is composed. These classes in turn remain empty terms if one does not know the factors on which they depend, *e.g.*, wage-labour, capital, and so on. These presuppose exchange, division of labour, prices, etc.[2]

Marx's model for scientific procedure clearly emphasizes theoretical generalities at the expense of concrete particulars.

Althusser's model for scientific procedure likewise emphasizes theoretical generalities – Generalities I, Generalities II and Generalities III. The scientist begins from Generalities I, a raw material of existing ideological interpretations of the world. He does *not* begin from directly observed concrete particulars, the raw material for science in the empiricist model: 'Contrary to the ideological illusions . . . of empiricism or sensualism, a science never works on an existence whose essence is pure immediacy and singularity ('sensations' or 'individuals'). . . . At its moment of constitution . . . a science always works on existing concepts.'[3] In Althusser's model, even the most immediate facts of experience have always already been interpreted – and interpreted, what's more, in a peculiarly untrustworthy way. For it is precisely the most immediate facts of experience that are most strongly influenced by self-interest and subjectivism. 'It is a peculiarity of every *ideological* conception . . . that it is governed by "interests" beyond the necessity of knowledge alone.'[4] For Althusser as for Spinoza, the lowest level of knowledge is when we think of everything in terms of our own experience (see especially the Appendix to Book I of Spinoza's *Ethics*). On this level, it seems quite natural and obvious that the sun is about 200 yards or so away from us in the sky.

In Althusser's model, the scientist passes beyond this level when he transforms the ideological interpretations of Generalities I into the genuine scientific knowledges of Generalities III by applying the proper methodological framework of Generalities II. There is still no infusion of concrete particulars; the whole process 'takes place *entirely in thought*'.[5] The knowledges of Generalities III are valid simply because produced by a Science that has been correctly set up: 'Once [sciences] are truly constituted and developed they have no need for verification from *external* practices to declare the knowledges they produce to be 'true' i.e., to be *knowledges* . . . they themselves provide the criterion of validity of their knowledges.'[6] Althusser even attempts to equate science with mathematics in this respect, drawing attention to the internal criteria by which results in mathematics are validated. Such an equation suggests the strangeness of Althusser's concept of Science; even so, Althusser still expects scientific procedure to do something that mathematical procedures could never do. For whereas results in mathematics are neither better nor worse than the postulates from which they logically derive, the scientific knowledges of Generalities III are a very definite improvement upon the ideological interpretations of Generalities I. When Althusser claims that Science can be unfolded out of Ideology, he is effectively claiming that Truth can be unfolded out of Error.

The key to the improvement, of course, is Generalities II. What is this '"theory" that defines the field in which all the problems of the science must necessarily be "posed"'?[7] Unfortunately, Althusser never describes it very clearly. Sometimes it seems that the scientist can convert Error into Truth solely by

the application of Marx's materialist dialectic. Thus Althusser
claims that 'the materialist dialectic [is] the sole method that
can anticipate . . . theoretical practice by drawing up its formal
conditions', and that 'the Theory . . . which transforms into
"knowledges" (scientific truths) the ideological product of
existing "empirical" practices . . . is the *materialist* dialectic'.[8]
At this point, the whole business begins to look like a mere
statement of blind Marxist faith. But a closer look at the specific
revolution wrought by Marx in the field of economics suggests a
rather wider version of Generalities II.

In the first place, it is plain that Marx's revolution in
economics was not built upon any large new accumulation of
directly observed evidence. Marx began from the existing
theories of Classical economics, exactly in accordance with
Althusser's model. What was revolutionary was Marx's new
perspective for looking at the experienced facts of those existing
theories – a higher perspective, moving outside of experience.
The Classical economists had experienced the facts of their own
contemporary bourgeois economic system as perfectly natural
and obvious and 'given'; they had observed what was *in front of*
their eyes, without ever being aware of the class-interest and
subjectivism that influenced such observation from *behind* their
eyes. Marx, however, posed 'the question of the "givenness" of
the object'.[9] He made economics aware of the ideological
position of the observer by querying 'not only the object of
[Classical] Political Economy, but also *Political Economy itself as
an object*'.[10] Althusser describes the revolution in Spinoza's
terminology: whereas the Classical economists had produced
only a science of 'conclusions', Marx now took into account the
'premises' that had influenced those 'conclusions'. What's
involved here is a reflexive move of thought that does indeed
take place entirely in thought. What's involved is the *move of the
critique*; and Althusser points to the significance of Marx's
subtitle for *Capital*: 'A Critique of Political Economy'.[11]

There is a similar move to be found in the history of many
other sciences. Althusser, following Engels, takes the example of
Lavoisier.[12] It was not by any large new accumulation of
directly observed evidence that Lavoisier discovered oxygen
and explained combustion; the evidence had already been observed by Priestley and Scheele. But these earlier chemists had

fitted the evidence into 'phlogiston' theory, a theory founded upon the assumption that fire is a *substance* which is *given off* by burning material. And, of course, this is exactly how fire does appear to experience. In order to discover oxygen and explain combustion, Lavoisier had to move outside of experience, and look at the experienced facts from a higher perspective. Similarly when Saussure directed the attention of linguists to 'langue' as an invisible object of study *behind* all actual speaking and writing; similarly when Einstein transformed the physicist's object of study by taking into account the spatio-temporal position of the observer. Clearly, Althusser's model for scientific procedure focuses upon something very important that the empiricist model all too often ignores.

Althusser's focus is very much in line with the traditional focus of Metaphysical philosophy. Hegel, in particular, uses the move of the critique to unfold the whole development of human thought (and to unfold his own philosophical system as a mirror of that development). Thus a critique of the concept of Being leads to the concept of Nothing; a critique of the concept of the One leads to the concept of the Many; and so on. For every new level of thought, Hegel reflects back upon a previous level, makes conscious its hidden premises, and takes into account what has been involved in thinking it. Hegel sees this unfolding as a kind of logic – and a more valuable logic than mathematical logic precisely because it unfolds something genuinely new, over and above its raw material.

(ii)

But it is one thing to recognize the importance of the critique, another thing to focus upon it to the exclusion of all else, as Hegel and Althusser do. For a logic that moves by critiques is not in the end a self-sufficient kind of logic. Unlike mathematical logic, it unfolds something genuinely new; but at the same time, it lacks the hard-and-fast necessity of mathematical logic. Unfortunately, Hegel and Althusser want both to eat their cake and have it. Thus Hegel claims an iron inevitability for his system, as though the only critique that could possibly be applied to the concept of Being is the critique that leads to the concept of Nothing, and as though the only critique that could possibly be applied to the concept of the One is the critique that leads to the concept of the Many. But could we not with a little ingenuity also manage to deduce the concept of the Many from the concept of Being? or the concept of Nothing from the concept of the One? Hegel's choice of the particular critique to be applied at a particular point is to some extent a free choice – a matter of relative plausibilities, if not of pure caprice. Certainly, we may well have doubts about the iron inevitability of a system of critiques which deduces Hegel's own philosophy as the ultimate mode of human thought, and the nineteenth-century Prussian monarchy – the source of Hegel's professorial salary – as the ultimate mode of social organization!

Althusser too fails to recognize the element of free choice in the move of the critique. Althusser talks about Generalities II as though there were just one single possible critique to be applied in any given field, one single critique to transform the level of ideological interpretation once and for all into the level of scientific knowledge. Such a view is quite blind to the history of science – or, at best, observes no more of the history of science than the great success stories. The real, full history of science is littered with unsuccessful critiques. One might mention Descartes's theory of vortices, or Goethe's colour theory – revolutionary higher perspectives that just happened to 'go up' in the wrong direction. It is true that science has consistently moved away from what seems natural and obvious to experience, but it does not follow that any move away from what seems natural and obvious to experience is thereby scientific.

If the move of the critique can 'go up' in various possible directions, it becomes necessary to evaluate the various possible theories produced by critiques. And here we come round to empiricism once again – a new kind of empiricism, making its claims in a new kind of place. The old kind of empiricism, 'naive' or Baconian empiricism, required the scientist to start off from concrete particulars before the level of interpretation, *before Generalities I*. We may grant Althusser's case against such empiricism. The new kind of empiricism, on the other hand, requires the scientist to return to concrete particulars after the level of theory, *after Generalities III*. This is Karl Popper's kind of empiricism. In Popper's model for scientific procedure, the scientist no longer attains to a theory by sheer accumulation of directly observed evidence; he might perfectly well develop a theory by making a critique of existing theories. But this theory is only a hypothesis until it has been checked and matched back against at least a sample of directly observed evidence.

There is no checking or matching back in Althusser's model for scientific procedure. For Althusser, the theoretical results of Generalities III are not hypotheses – but already, infallibly, knowledges. No need for such knowledges to hark back to real things in the outside world! Althusser dismisses the notion of truth as a correspondence between ideas and things. Following Spinoza again, he insists that 'the *object* of knowledge or essence [is] in itself absolutely distinct and different from the *real object*'.[13] (He also borrows Spinoza's entirely inappropriate *mathematical* example, of the difference between the idea of a circle and a circle as a real object.) Ideas and things are, simply, worlds apart: 'There is no common homogenous space (spirit or real) between the abstract of the concept of a thing and the empirical concrete of this thing.'[14] In Althusser's model for scientific procedure, knowledge is never *about* the outside world at all.

But if knowledge is never *about* the outside world, then the outside world is unknowable to us; and if the outside world is unknowable to us, then as far as we are concerned it might just as well not exist. Although Althusser continues to talk about the 'real-concrete' of an independent outside world, the 'real-concrete' has no justifiable reason to exist in his philosophy. Like Kant's ill-fated 'Ding an Sich', the 'real-concrete' is a mere survival from non-philosophical common sense. Its logical irrelevance has already been pointed out (from differing angles) by Benton, Lovell, and Hindess and Hirst.[15]

But even as he drives the *real* out into the cold, Althusser tries to let the *concrete* in through the back door. In place of the 'real-concrete', he inserts the 'concept-concrete'. The 'concept-concrete' is generated out of Generalities III, not as a concretion to which theoretical results refer, but as a concretion of results themselves. Althusser thus claims for his Science the kind of superiority which we ordinarily attribute to science when we see it as more solidly based upon concrete evidence than ideology; but Althusser does not pay for such superiority in empiricist coin. In the 'concept-concrete', concretion has become a property quite detached from its primary home in the outside world – and from its secondary home in the 'concrete' images of memory or imagination. In the 'concept-concrete', concretion has become a very mysterious property altogether.

What Althusser has in mind, it seems, is what Marx had in mind when he made the claim that 'the concrete concept is concrete because it is a synthesis of many definitions'.[16] Such a claim is very much in line with Metaphysical philosophy. Traditionally, Metaphysical philosophers generate concretion by an *intersection* of Forms or Categories or Modes and Attributes; thus, what we know as a pebble is generated by an intersection of concepts of Hardness, Roundness, Smallness, etc. In similar fashion, the scientist envisages a particular situation in mechanical physics as an intersection of concepts of Gravity, Mass, Friction, etc. But for Metaphysical philosophers, of course, the concretion of the pebble is the concretion of what we know as the real outside world (albeit a very unusual version of the real outside world). On this point, Althusser explicitly disassociates himself from even the Objective variety of Idealism.[17] For Althusser, the intersection of concepts – as of Gravity, Mass, Friction, etc. – only ever generates a conceptual situation, never a real situation. Althusser therefore tries to discard the claim to reality whilst retaining the claim to concretion. But the latter claim dissolves without the former. For the intersection of concepts does not produce concretion *per se*; it produces only particulars, which Metaphysical philosophers can interpret as concrete particulars only because they interpret them as realities. When the scientist envisages a particular situation of intersecting Gravity, Mass, Friction, etc., this situation may be highly specific and determinate and individualized – but until it refers to (or converts to) the real outside world, it still exists entirely in the abstract.

Althusser, in effect, only uses the word 'concrete' after knocking all the solid stuffing out of it. Similarly with the word 'materialism'. Amongst Marxists, philosophical materialism is of course obligatory; but when Althusser lays claim to 'materialism', he deprives the word of all its ordinary meaning. Consider his proposal for 'a critical, i.e. a materialist' reading of Lenin's Notes on reading Hegel. According to Althusser, Lenin does not turn Hegel into a materialist by the orthodox inversion of 'put[ting] matter in place of the Idea and *vice versa*' – 'for that would merely produce a new materialist metaphysics (i.e. a materialist version of classical philosophy, say, at best a mechanistic materialism)'; instead, Lenin turns Hegel into a materialist simply by reading him from 'a proletarian *class viewpoint* (a dialectical-materialist viewpoint)'.[18] With this method of reading, even Hegel's Absolute Idea can be made to reveal a 'materialist kernel'.[19]

There seems only one way to make sense of 'materialism' in this context – viz., by arguing that a reading from the proletarian class viewpoint is a reading directed towards practical political action, and that practical political action has a *material* effect upon the world. Such an argument would also make sense of Althusser's obscure notion of 'concern' in the assertion that 'of course, [the concept-concrete] does concern the concrete-real'.[20] But this is not a *scientific* kind of materialism; this is a *religious* kind of materialism, characteristic of any system of thought which sees not what the world *is* but what it *must be*. On such an argument, Mohammedanism can also count as a materialism. In the end, Althusser's version of Science seems to fall back upon a blind Marxist faith after all.

9
Foucault as archaeologist

Foucault carries Althusser's position through to more extreme conclusions. Like Althusser, he rejects the notion of truth as a matching or correspondence of ideas to things, and, like Althusser, he rejects the traditional belief that western science has been advancing towards this kind of truth. But unlike Althusser, he does not take it for granted that western science must still have been advancing in some other sort of way. Instead, he rejects the traditional belief in scientific progress.

In so doing, he rejects the traditional teleological version of scientific history which Althusser also takes for granted. The teleological version of scientific history focuses upon those past discoveries and knowledges which still seem important to us nowadays, those past discoveries and knowledges which can be seen as beating a path up to our own door. (In similar vein, a teleological version of political history might tell everything that happened to the German races from the Fall of the Roman Empire to 1871 in terms of a progress towards German nation-hood.) But Foucault tries to see past periods through their own eyes, without retrospective selection. And he takes into account not just those past discoveries and knowledges which still seem important to us nowadays, but also and equally those past discoveries and knowledges which seem quite bizarre and incredible to us nowadays. Foucault's 'archaeological' version of scientific history is a fascinating recovery of all the discards and failures and forgotten areas of human thought.

What this recovery reveals is that even the most apparently 'superstitious' period still makes perfectly good sense of the world in its own kind of way. (In this respect, Foucault demonstrates for historically remote societies what Lévi-Strauss demonstrates for geographically remote societies.) And, conversely, even the most apparently 'scientific' period is still perfectly irrational about the world in its own kind of way. There is no decisive revolution from ideology to science – neither the long-term revolution envisaged in most histories of human thought, nor the all-at-once revolution envisaged by Althusser. There is simply a succession of different ideologies, some of which consider themselves 'scientific'. (If Foucault himself prefers to avoid the term 'ideology', this is mainly in order to avoid any suggestion that ideology is something false and something different to science.)

Foucault's attitude to 'scientific' revolutions is clearly demonstrated in his account of the advent of modern medical science around the end of the eighteenth century. Ordinarily, we would think of this as a triumphant breakthrough from ignorance to truth. But Foucault presents it very differently. According to Foucault, the old 'superstitious' medicine made perfectly good sense of disease – but in terms of a discourse which has since been banished and forgotten. This discourse framed disease against a dominant assumption of life; and against a dominant assumption of life, disease showed up as a counter-life, an evil, a negative force. Disease was always the invisible 'other' of the visible human body. But in the new discourse emerging around the end of the eighteenth century, disease shows up not as a negative force but as a positive object – a positive object for a positivist science to study. Disease is no longer the invisible 'other' of the visible human body, but something visible in its own right *inside* the human body. It is no coincidence that the end of the eighteenth century also sees the emergence of pathological anatomy, the practice of opening up bodies in order to inspect disease actually within the organs. But this practice, of course, can only be carried out upon *dead* bodies. So in this respect, the new discourse frames disease against a dominant assumption of death. As Foucault puts it: 'Disease breaks away from the metaphysic of evil, to which it had been related for centuries; and it finds in the visibility of death the full form in which its content appears in positive terms.'[1] Even to think and speak about disease in terms of separate static internal organs presupposes death as 'the concrete a priori of medical experience'.[2]

When Foucault puts it like this, the advent of modern medical science no longer looks like a case of scales falling from before the eyes:

> It is as if for the first time for thousands of years, doctors, free at last of theories and chimeras, agreed to approach the object of their experience with the purity of an unprejudiced gaze. But the analysis must be turned around: it is the forms of visibility that have changed; the new medical spirit . . . is nothing more than a syntactical reorganization of disease in which the limits of the visible and invisible follow a new pattern.[3]

The object that modern medical science studies no longer appears as something natural and obvious; on the contrary, it has to be carved literally or mentally out of the body, by an unnatural act of violence against the body. Nor was this object always there and waiting to be discovered; on the contrary, it has to be created by a certain practice – of pathological anatomy – and a certain way of speaking – in terms of separate static internal organs. (It is the combination of a practice and a way of speaking that constitutes what Foucault calls a discourse: not just a language, but also the 'experimental' approach which supports that language.) The vaunted objectivity of 'scientific' method here consists of turning the human body into an object for being objective about.

Of course, we might still want to argue against Foucault that, even if modern medical discourse is heavy with assumption and not transparent at all, it has none the less been proved valid in the long run by the success of its results. But on Foucault's argument, a discourse itself furnishes the very criteria by which its results are judged successful. And certainly, there have been growing suspicions in recent years that the much-vaunted achievements of modern medical science are, by other criteria, somehow missing the point. Thus there have been growing suspicions about the long-term implications of the 'Magic Bullet' approach to curing infections, about the psychological implications of the 'hygienic' approach to childbirth, about the moral implications of the 'human vegetable' approach to maintaining bodily functions at all costs, and so on. Are we not here witnessing the final consequences of a way of looking at the body as though it were dead? Modern medical science has evidently produced its own kind of blindnesses along with its own kind of visibilities.

The self-confirming nature of modern medical science appears even more plainly when it extends its sway from bodily health to mental health. In Foucault's description, psychiatric medicine depends overwhelmingly upon the prestige and authority accorded to the figure of the doctor in our society. Thus the new 'medical' attitude to mental 'disease', as promoted by Tuke and Pinel also around the end of the eighteenth century, 'did not introduce science but a personality, whose powers borrowed from science only their disguise, or at most their justification'.[4] In effect, psychiatric medicine works only to the extent that patients are persuaded into speaking a scientific language about themselves. Patients are 'mad' because they have evaded the primary socialization which ordinarily enters into human beings along with their society's language; but they can still be subdued and at least partially socialized by a secondary web of restraining language. Needless to say, this seemingly 'successful' result in no way proves the validity of the psychiatrist's language. The psychiatrist has not caught the truth of madness in his language, he has merely taught it to speak the same language back to him. 'What we call psychiatric practice is a certain moral tactic . . . overlaid by the myths of positivism.'[5] Once again, this is a kind of objectivity that first creates its object for being objective about.

In general, Foucault views the science of modern medicine in much the same way as we ordinarily view the 'science' of wine-buffery. For the object that wine-buffs study is not at all natural or obvious, it was not always there waiting to be discovered. Without the special wine-buffs' language (of 'rounded', 'smooth', 'full-bodied', etc.) and without the special wine-buffs' practices (of holding wine in the mouth in ways that separate out the 'palate' from the 'finish', etc.), our experience of the taste and smell of wine is quite shapeless and transient, impossible to pin down or recall voluntarily after the event. (Everyday language does not help because it offers so very few words for categorizing tastes and smells.) But with this special language and these special practices, wine-buffs – as a mutually supportive society – create an object for being objective about. And their results are certainly successful by their own criteria: a genuine expert, at least, can recognize wines with remarkable accuracy. None the less, the prestige and authority accorded to this discourse drives out other equally possible, equally valid discourses. For instance, a different approach with a different language and practices could define the experience of wine in social or religious terms – a Bacchic definition of wine. By other criteria, the wine-buff's discourse quite misses the point of the experience.

(ii)

In Foucault's 'archaeological' history, the advent of modern medical science around the end of the eighteenth century ties in with a whole range of similar transformations in human thought. Doctors and psychiatrists were able to constitute their own particular 'scientific' object under a new conceptual framework – and a new version of objectivity – that spread across the general community of scientists around the end of the eighteenth century. Such large-scale conceptual frameworks, which Foucault calls 'epistēmēs', are the ultimate revelation of 'archaeological' history.

An epistēmē, as Foucault describes it, is a social *a priori* of a kind that precedes any possible original discovery and any possible truth to the world. It precedes any possible original discovery because it is social and must therefore be spoken *together* before it can be spoken individually. 'One can no longer say that a discovery . . . inaugurates . . . a new phase in the history of discourse.'[6] And it precedes any possible truth to the world because it is an *a priori* and must therefore constitute the very ground upon which truth and falsity can be debated. Foucault does not deny that theories may be more or less true and more or less original within an epistēmē. Within an epistēmē, he proposes quite as much conflict and disagreement between opposing theories as we ordinarily allow for. But between epistēmēs, he proposes something much more than we ordinarily allow for: a discontinuity so deep and unbridgeable as to be beyond even conflict and disagreement.

Such is the vision of 'archaeological' history. There are no absolute foundations of human thought; the foundations change from one epistēmē to another. So, whereas the orthodox history of human thought is a history of the different things that have been seen in the world by human eyes, 'archaeological' history is a history of the different worlds that different human eyes have seen. Foucault's achievement is to give us, for a moment, those different eyes, and have us realize, for a moment, how natural and obvious a different world can seem through them.

The Hegelian analogy emerges very plainly here. For Hegel too proposed a history that would deal with something more than things in the world – a 'philosophical' history as distinct from the 'anti-universal', 'pragmatic', 'critical' and 'fragmentary' varieties of factual history. And he developed the outlines of such a history in his account of the very general frameworks, or *Zeitgeists*, that have dominated the successive periods of human thought. Thus the thought of the Roman period, according to Hegel, was dominated by the concept of Law. Of course, Hegel's *Zeitgeists* are crudely homogenous and oversimplified compared to Foucault's epistēmēs – after all, Hegel was always more of a philosopher than a historian. But Hegel, following Schiller, did none the less recognize very radical changes in the foundations of human thought; and, even more than Schiller, he had the imagination to envisage historical worlds utterly different to our own.

In this historicism, Hegel differs significantly from Plato and Spinoza. By objectifying his objective ideas in social customs and institutions, Hegel makes them dependent upon a given state of society. Hegel's Objective Idealism is not a philosophy of perfect, timeless, immutable *idealities* – quite the contrary. Hegel *relativizes* the concept of the *a priori*. Admittedly, he still sees the historical succession of *Zeitgeists* marching towards a final perfect immutable state that embodies the Absolute Idea. But there is a potential for irrationalism in his kind of rationalism. And this potential was in fact very strongly brought out by the most influential twentieth-century French proponent of Hegelianism, Alexander Kojève.[7] In Kojève's interpretation of Hegel, the progression from *Zeitgeist* to *Zeitgeist* depends more upon social might than intellectual right, and there are no absolute standards of reality at all: what was true in one period can become false in another period, and what was false in one period can become true in another.

The potential for irrationalism is present in Superstructuralism too, right from the very start. Durkheim is a case in point. In Durkheim's highly social conception of the *a priori*, the rational thought of a given society can only be built upon foundations which are unthought and irrational. In the case of primitive societies, such foundations take the form of religious belief; in the case of our own present-day society, they take the form of a belief in science:

> It is not enough that [concepts] be true to be believed. If they are not in harmony with the other beliefs and opinions, or, in a word, with the mass of the other collective representations, they will be denied; minds will be closed to them; consequently it will be as though they did not exist. Today it is generally sufficient that they bear the stamp of science to receive a sort of privileged credit, because we have faith in science. But this faith does not differ essentially from religious faith . . . science rests upon opinion.[8]

Even when science (presumably in the human sciences) manages to observe its own underlying irrationality, it still cannot free itself from opinion:

> It is undoubtedly true that this opinion can be taken as the object of a study and a science made of it. . . . But the science of opinion does not make opinions; it can only observe them and make them more conscious of themselves. It is true that by this means it can lead them to change, but science continues to be dependent upon opinion at the very moment when it seems to be making its laws.[9]

There is a very obvious anticipation of Foucault here.

Durkheim similarly anticipates Foucault on the subject of those who do not conform to their society's social *a priori*. In

Hegel's philosophy, of course, the possibility of non-conformity is not even recognized. But Durkheim recognizes the possibility, and recognizes society's way of dealing with it: 'Does a mind ostensibly free itself from these forms of thought? It is no longer considered a human mind in the full sense of the word, and is treated accordingly.'[10] This brief insight foretells all of Foucault's excavations into the unrecorded and unrecordable side of history, into the existences of those who are excluded and denied the right to their discourse. The mind that does not conform is treated as aberrational, as mad, as perverted.

But if Durkheim and Foucault see the same facts, yet they take diametrically opposite attitudes towards them. Durkheim, with his curiously conservative 'socialisme', is quite happy to replace the principle of truth with a principle of social morality, quite happy to believe that science is valid for us because our society is valid for us. Nor does he feel any compunction about sacrificing non-conformists upon the altar of social solidarity – in spite of the fact that the thought of the judges is fundamentally just as irrational as the thought of the victims. Foucault, on the other hand, identifies with the victims. He identifies with them, not because their discourse would be *more* true, but because it would be no *less* true, and yet they are made to suffer for it. And he is hostile towards modern science, not because any alternative would be *more* objective, but because modern science proclaims and dismisses any alternative as *less* objective.

Indeed, Foucault seems happier with periods of history when social coercion was at least visible and overt. What he resents about the modern period in western history is that, thanks to modern science, social coercion has become insidious. For science excludes the non-conformists and denies them the right to their discourse, whilst all the time pretending to be pure and impartial and disinterested. Oppression by the smug superiority of 'knowledge' is particularly oppressive. Foucault has no more *reason* for attacking modern science and modern society than Durkheim has for endorsing them. But it is very evident in Foucault's 'archaeological' history that, although he cannot view any epistēmē as objectively better or worse than any other, yet he *feels* much more favourably towards pre- or post-scientific epistēmēs than towards scientific ones.

(iii)

Foucault's most complete history of epistēmēs is in *The Order of Things*. Here we have the four major epistēmēs of the last five centuries: Renaissance, Classical, Modern, and Post-Modern cum Structuralist. (These periods are in fact much like those in any other history of thought, save in the lack of a crucial revolution at the start of the twentieth century; Foucault's Structuralist period begins only tentatively with Freud and Saussure, and is still in the process of arriving.) *The Order of Things* also presents Foucault's most general and wide-ranging history of epistēmēs. For Foucault here examines not just one scientific field but the interrelations between three fields; and he readily refers to analogous developments in philosophy, literature and other sciences.

The three fields examined in *The Order of Things* are the study of language, the study of economic exchange and the study of living organisms. As usual in Foucault's 'archaeological' history, the focus is upon sciences less surely established than the 'hard' natural sciences, and sciences which have a particularly strong bearing on man's own idea of himself. And, as usual, the objects that these sciences study turn out to be quite different from epistēmē to epistēmē. Thus, the Modern period understands language, economic exchange and living organisms in a very different sense to the Classical period; and the further development of psychological and anthropological perspectives in the Modern period yields further new objects. It is only under these later perspectives that the truly 'human' human sciences emerge. And such human sciences are themselves dehumanized – or about to be dehumanized – in the Post-Modern period.

As regards the Renaissance period, there are no human sciences because there is no specifically human object of knowledge. In this epistēmē, the division between the human and the non-human does not exist. Foucault's Renaissance stands at the tail-end of the theological Middle Ages, and, by way of God, turns the whole world into a cultural product. What we now see as the natural world appears in the Renaissance as a great artifice, a great book, in which God, as the Word itself, inscribes signs and clues and an endless play of overlapping resemblances for men to interpret. (For a similar account of the Renaissance world, see E. M. W. Tillyard's book, *The Elizabethan World Picture*.) And, as the natural world is a kind of language, so human language is a kind of nature. Thus the fables of extraordinary plants and animals handed down in books are just as reliable in the way of evidence as any first-hand observation of plants and animals. What appears to us nowadays merely as an incredible degree of subservience to 'authority' is really the consequence of a totally different epistemological framework. In the Renaissance, language is not regarded as a secondary human creation always liable to diverge from the primary world; it is 'a part of the world, ontologically interwoven with it'.[11]

With the rise of the natural sciences in the early part of the seventeenth century, the Renaissance gives way to the Classical period. In this new period, the non-human splits off from the human. There is a sharp and simple dichotomy: the natural world becomes an object to be known by the human mind as a subject. But, at the same time, this knowing operates in a very close and immediate way, holding subject and object directly up against each other, face to face. Specifically, this knowing operates as *representation*: the mind re-presents a simulacrum of the outside world. Or, in a favourite metaphor of the Classical period, the outside world is captured in the mind like a reflection in a mirror. What's more, this knowing is essentially optical, just as the metaphor suggests. According to Foucault, the Classical notion of first-hand observation devolves upon a single human sense – the sense of sight. And the understanding that accompanies such observation is no more than a kind of visual analysis, articulating a general picture into its component parts and features. Hence the predilection for classificatory tables and taxonomies in the Classical period. Although the non-human and the human have split apart, there is still an assumed harmony between them, which makes it very easy for the mind to take down the true pattern of things.

This Classical dichotomy is well suited to the development of the 'hard' natural sciences, where the world of the object is non-human Nature and the world of the human subject is pure transparency. But it also allows a development of the 'softer' sciences of life and culture, to the extent that they can fit into the same mould. Thus the Classical study of economic exchange is founded upon a somewhat limited concept of wealth, where wealth is something in Nature – i.e. land – or at least something visually observable – i.e. goods. Similarly in the study of living organisms. Classical Natural History describes plants and animals (and not man) in terms of their visually observable parts and features; it is, in Foucault's words, 'nothing more than the nomination of the visible'.[12] As for the study of language, the Classical view is that language should be no more than the transparent glass over the reflecting silver of the mind. The business of language is to let the picture through, and to let the picture re-reflect from mind to mind, with a minimum of interference and distortion. Thus viewed, language becomes a mere passive application of names. 'The fundamental task of Classical "discourse" is *to ascribe a name to things, and in that name to name their being*.'[13] In the final total taxonomy of the world, the pattern of names in language will harmonize with the pattern of representations in the mind which will harmonize with the pattern of things in Nature.

Around the end of the eighteenth century, however, this kind of harmony begins to seem no longer attainable. In the natural sciences, for instance, the focus shifts from the mechanical interactions of solid bodies to the insubstantial functionings of forces like electricity, heat and magnetism; and Nature ceases to be an 'object' in the simple thing-like sense of the term. First-hand observation still allows one to record the effects of electricity, heat and magnetism, but it does not allow one to picture the forces as they are in themselves. The forces as they are in themselves have become inaccessible to the sense of sight; they can be known only by the understanding, only in the abstract. 'The visible order with its permanent grid of distinctions, is now only a superficial glitter above an abyss.'[14] In the natural sciences, the reality of Nature retreats outside the ambit of man's mirroring apparatus, just as, in philosophy (and also around the end of the eighteenth century), the Kantian thing-in-itself vanishes beyond the bounds of knowledge.

Likewise in the study of language, economic exchange and living organisms, the new epistémē brings to light the functioning of abstract forces outside of man's direct experience. In economics, for instance, the observable substance of goods turns out to be merely a surface manifestation of something which cannot be directly observed, something which is 'hidden' in the past history of the goods – namely, the force of human labour expended in their production. The truth about economic exchange is that the activity is the measure of the things. But as Marx most notably demonstrates, this truth is inaccessible to ordinary experience, which knows exchange only in terms of goods. Similarly in the study of living organisms. The outward parts and features turn out to be merely a surface manifestation of the essential inward organs; and the organs themselves, 'which are spatial, solid, directly or indirectly visible', have to be understood by way of 'the functions, which are not perceptible, but determine, as though from below, the arrangement of what we do perceive'.[15] No longer does one account for a living organism by finding its place in a taxonomic table; now one accounts for it in terms of a past history of internal growth. This kind of thinking, when applied to the totality of all living species, leads to the Darwinian conept of a 'hidden' past history of evolution.

As for the study of language, the nineteenth century sees the advent of historical philology. The Classical dream of a single great pattern of names is overthrown; now there is a multitude of separate languages, all with their own peculiar evolutionary histories, like so many separate living species. And, by virtue of their own peculiar evolutionary histories, these separate languages all have their own peculiar deposits of vocabulary and grammar – thus determining the possibilities of what can be expressed in them. As Foucault puts it on behalf of the new epistēmē:

> Expressing their thoughts in words of which they are not the masters, enclosing them in verbal forms whose historical dimensions they are unaware of, men believe that their speech is their servant and do not realize that they are submitting themselves to its demands. The grammatical arrangements of a language are the *a priori* of what can be expressed in it.[16]

Language is no longer a pure transparency, but filled with 'hidden' forces that the language-user never directly experiences.

In these 'softer' sciences of life and culture, the notion of abstract forces has an effect which it does not have in the natural sciences: it bends back round against the notion of the human subject. Suddenly man finds himself under the control of his own language and biology and economic system. The abstract forces are 'exterior to himself, and older than his own birth', they 'anticipate him, overhang him with all their solidity, and traverse him as though he were merely an object of nature'.[17] No longer can man hold himself aloof and superior. With the new notion of abstract forces, the Classical dichotomy between the subject as mirror and the object as thing has become irrelevant. For the same abstract forces run through *both* the human subject *and* the non-human object; and the human subject is inserted back in with the rest of the world again.

From Foucault's point of view, this is all a step in the right direction. But it is compromised, in the Modern period, by a simultaneous step in the wrong direction. For the Modern period, according to Foucault, invents a new image of man that recuperates his importance and apartness: the image of psychological man. Psychological man retreats inwardly out of the reach of the forces which control his outward language and labour; he dwells privately in the middle of his own purely individual experience. Such inwardness was never even contemplated in the Renaissance and Classical periods. But it arises in the nineteenth century as a general cultural trend (with the Romantic poets, for instance, and the psychological nineteenth-century novelists); and it is visible as a general philosophical trend in the 'I'-philosophies of Rousseau and Kant, the Phenomenologists and the Existentialists.

According to Foucault, these general trends lie behind the nineteenth-century creation of the truly 'human' human sciences – anthropology, sociology and, of course, psychology itself. (Unfortunately, it is often difficult to know exactly what sciences Foucault has in mind, because the relevant chapters, 'Man and His Doubles' and 'The Human Sciences', do not refer to specific anthropologists, sociologists, psychologists or other human scientists in the way that previous chapters referred to Condillac, Turgot, Linnaeus, Smith, Cuvier, Bopp, etc. Foucault's discussion of the new human sciences remains always more of a discussion of the general cultural and philosophical trends that have influenced them.) The new human sciences counter the move by which the non-human object, in philology, biology and nineteenth-century economics, bends back round and dehumanizes the subject; in the new human sciences, the human subject swings across and constitutes itself on the side of the object. So, as the Classical dichotomy fails, a new dichotomy appears – a dichotomy not between the human and the non-human, but within the human itself. And, within the human itself, subject and object can come directly up against each other, face-to-face once more; for man's experience is still directly observable, even if the forces 'hidden' behind it are not. Thus the Classical situation is restored in a new mode, and 'it is easy to understand why every time one tries to use the human sciences to philosophize . . . one finds oneself imitating the philosophical posture of the eighteenth century, in which, nevertheless, man had no place.'[18] What's more, there is even a possibility of restoring the Classical ideal of totality, the single great pattern, in a new mode. For is not every kind of knowledge also a psychological experience? Could one not draw together under a single conspectus a psychology of mathematics, a psychology of optical observation, a psychology of philosophy, and so on and so forth? Man's inward retreat is beginning to look like a master-tactic for securing the ultimate victory.

But the further development of anthropology and psychology turns the tables on man once again. In the Post-Modern cum Structuralist period, a new abstract force of signs and signification appears, a force not recognized under the positivistic framework of the nineteenth century. When this new abstract force enters into Freud's psychoanalysis and Lévi-Strauss's ethnology, even the human sciences of psychology and anthropology can no longer claim to understand man on the basis of his own experience. In Foucault's words, 'Not only are [psychoanalysis and ethnology] able to do without the concept of man, they are also unable to pass through it. . . . One may say of both of them . . . that they dissolve man.'[19] At the same time, there is the further Saussurean development of linguistics, which extends the control of language until it penetrates into even the most private thoughts and representations. Under the Post-Modern epistēmē, man is routed from his final bastion of psychological inwardness. The abstract forces that first threatened to overrun him in biology, philology and nineteenth-century economics can no longer be staved off. The dichotomy of subject and object begins to fail in *every* mode; and the attitude of aloofness and superiority that man has so long maintained towards the rest of the world begins to slip irretrievably away from him.

However, it seems that these implications of the Post-Modern epistēmē are still to be fully realized. In dealing with the Post-Modern epistēmē, Foucault is not just recounting the past but also predicting the future; and not just predicting the future but also promoting one possible future in preference to others. (Thus Structuralism appears in a much less promising light when yoked alongside phenomenology in the 'Man and His Doubles' chapter.) In the chapter on 'The Human Sciences', the Post-Modern epistēmē is presented as a goal that we are on the verge of achieving. And Foucault hereby reveals an undeniable teleological drift. Although the theory of epistēmēs apparently involves an acceptance of pure haphazard change from period to period, yet the actual history of epistēmēs ends up by pushing human thought towards a goal that Foucault quite clearly desires.

In fact, the actual history of epistēmēs has never really been haphazard at all. From period to period, each epistēmē *answers to* and *rises upon* its predecessor – though it may not necessarily *improve upon it*. *The Order of Things* presents a Grand Historical Design of impeccable and inevitable logic, working through a dialectical succession of divisions and reunifications. Thus the monism of the Renaissance period is separated out in the Classical period into a first division of subject-versus-object; this subject-versus-object division is closed over in the Modern period, but only as an alternative subject-versus-object division is separated out; finally, this alternative subject-versus-object division is itself closed over in the new monism of the Post-Modern period. Of course, there is no progress towards truth in the scientific sense here, no progress towards a true subject-to-object matching of ideas to things. But there is a progress towards what Foucault evidently regards as the philosophical truth of monism, where subject and object are inseparable – and therefore unmatchable. After the initial fall from monism, brought on by science in the seventeenth century, human thought cycles inevitably round – even by way of science itself – to a final recovery of monism in the Post-Modern period.

Again, the Hegelian analogy stares us in the face. For Hegel too, the history of human thought has a logic of its own, a logic which proceeds through a dialectical succession of divisions and reunifications, regardless of man's conscious intentions. And for Hegel too, this logic must lead in the end to the philosophical truth of monism. The scientific kind of truth is no more than a step along the way (though Hegel does not bear towards it anything like Foucault's animus); the ultimate truth lies not in any subject-to-object matching of ideas to things, but, on the contrary, in the ultimate inseparability of subject and object. A century and a half before Foucault, Hegel already believed that this ultimate truth was about to arrive.

(iv)

Still, there are differences between Hegel and Foucault, and very important ones. As regards the logic of history, for instance, Hegel claims that each new *Zeitgeist* incorporates what was of value in its predecessor. Like a single thinking consciousness, human thought successively transcends its own perspectives, yet still continues to see from its latest highest perspective all that the previous perspectives saw. By the logic of the Hegelian *Aufhebung*, nothing is ever ultimately lost. But by Foucault's logic, nothing is ever ultimately saved. Foucault insists that the history of human thought 'cannot be reduced to the general model of a consciousness that acquires, progresses, and remembers'.[20] Only from the uniquely all-encompassing standpoint of the 'archaeological' historian can it be seen that each new epistēmē answers to its predecessor; the thinkers actually within an epistēmē see nothing of what previous epistēmēs saw. The Classical period simply forgets the Renaissance perspective, the Modern period simply forgets the Classical perspective, and so on. No understanding ever passes across the abyss between epistēmēs.

There is a corresponding difference in the goals that Hegel and Foucault envisage for human thought. For Hegel, the final phase of monism incorporates all the previous achievements of science and subject-to-object knowing; it casts them under a new perspective, certainly, but it still has a place for them. But for Foucault, the final phase of monism is thoroughly anti-scientific. Hence his interpretation of Freudian psychoanalysis:

> Whereas all the human sciences advance towards the uncon-scious only with their back to it, waiting for it to unveil itself as fast as consciousness is analysed, psychoanalysis, on the other hand, points directly towards it . . . towards what exists with the mute solidity of a thing, of a text closed in upon itself, or of a blank space in a visible text.[21]

In the end, the Unconscious is not just beyond the conscious-ness of the individual patient, but beyond anyone's conscious-ness. Thus Foucault goes on to describe the 'invincible torture' that schizophrenic madness represents for the psychoanalyst: 'psycho-analysis "recognizes itself" when it is confronted with those very psychoses which . . . it has scarcely any means of reaching'.[22] The light that was to have been shed upon the object falls back upon the subject; and instead of a new depth of understanding, there is only the recognition of the impossibility of understanding. Clearly, the implications of psychoanalysis – still to be fully realized in the Post-Modern epistēmē – are far beyond anything that Freud himself realized.

The terminology of 'mute solidity' and 'blank space' is typical of Foucault's way of describing the Post-Modern apotheosis. Whereas Hegel arrives at monism in the form of the Absolute Idea, Foucault arrives at monism as a kind of absolute density and opacity, a kind of Absolute Being. And whereas Hegel slants monism in favour of the mind – until even things are drawn in and made luminous with spirit – Foucault slants monism in favour of thingish-ness – until the mind is driven back upon itself and finally squeezed out of existence. Or again: whereas Hegel makes monism into a triumph of self-identity – in the sense that human thought ultimately identifies the uni-verse with itself – Foucault makes monism into a triumph of the 'radically other' – in the sense that the universe is ultimately ruled by alien forces of unconsciousness and non-consciousness, even by Death.[23] For Foucault, human thought develops towards the goal of its own extinction.

Needless to say, this puts human thought into a highly

paradoxical state, and creates problems that Hegel never had to encounter. The problems are the traditional problems of any philosophy which leads knowing to a knowledge of ultimate unknowability, and thereupon summons knowing to un-know itself – as by an active forgetting, as by Nietzsche's 'aktive Vergesslichkeit'. Unfortunately for such philosophies, unknowing is something that only happens to us from the outside; it can never be a *consequence* of knowing. We can no more know ourselves into un-knowing than we can consciously make ourselves go to sleep or consciously make ourselves cease to remember a piece of information. To know the utter ineffectuality of consciousness does not render us one whit the less conscious. On the contrary, the more consciousness knows good reasons for its own extinction, the further it is from becoming extinct. When Foucault summons knowing to un-know itself, he is actually summoning it to a perpetual oscillation between two extremes of consciousness and unconsciousness.

In fact, Foucault conceives the thought of the Post-Modern epistēmē – when it finally fully realizes itself – neither as a rational knowledge nor as a blind oblivion, but rather as a kind of mysticism. Towards the end of *The Order of Things*, for instance, he has intimations of 'a mode of thought, unknown hitherto in our culture, that will make it possible to reflect at the same time, without discontinuity or contradiction, upon man's being and the being of language'.[24] He also hopes for 'a total reabsorption of all forms of discourse into a single word, of all books into a single page, of the whole world into one book'; and he suggests that 'thought . . . is about to re-apprehend itself in its entirety, and to illumine itself once more in the lightning flash of being'.[25] Clearly, he is in search of some instantaneous glimpsing insight that can encompass both knowing and unknowing; equally clearly, he is finding such insight very difficult to locate in any meaningful terms.

In so far as he does locate such insight meaningfully, he does so in terms of modern literature. The single-word single-page single-book theme has been a favourite ever since Mallarmé, for instance; and so, more importantly, has the theme of non-representational language. Recent French literature, especially that produced under the influence of the *Tel Quel* group, has particularly sought to present words in all their absolute density and opacity, so that 'what is speaking is . . . in its nothingness, the word itself – not the meaning of the word, but its enigmatic and precarious being'.[26] Such solid and unconscious words defeat all ordinary knowing and consciousness *through* language; yet they still 'speak' by bringing about a kind of instantaneous glimpsing insight into the ultimate rule of solidity and unconsciousness. So far so good: literature can directly embody un-knowing, where cognitive language can proceed only by way of knowing. But it still needs to be added that this embodied un-knowing will 'speak' only to the reader who has already been philosophically prepared for it. The actual *Tel Quel* literature depends to a peculiar degree upon an extra-literary knowing of the *Tel Quel* theories and *Tel Quel* literary criticism. The unprepared reader is more likely to dismiss non-representational language as a mere particular case of non-sense, in no way insightful or illuminating.

The paradoxical state of the Post-Modern epistēmē becomes doubly paradoxical in relation to Foucault himself. For if all human thought necessarily belongs within some framing epistēmē, then Foucault's 'archaeological' thought presumably ought to belong with the Post-Modern epistēmē. But Foucault's 'archaeological' thought is not literature; it works through cognitive language to produce ordinary knowing and consciousness. And what it knows and brings into consciousness is precisely what, on Foucault's own account, no thought within an epistēmē can ever know or bring into consciousness: namely, the history of previous epistēmēs. For on Foucault's own account, every epistēmē irretrievably forgets the thought of its predecessors. Consequently, the supremely elevated and encompassing consciousness of 'archaeological' history must be outside of any possible epistēmē. The self-contradiction is glaring and obvious. Hegel did not encounter it because his own Hegelian consciousness of all previous *Zeitgeists* was perfectly compatible with – was indeed an essential component of – the final super-consciousness of the Absolute Idea. But Foucault's 'archaeological' history is precluded by the very terms of the philosophy of 'archaeological' history itself.

Foucault recognizes the difficulty at the end of *The Archaeology of Knowledge*, when he attributes the following objection to an imaginary body of phenomenologically oriented historians:

What . . . is the title of your discourse? Where does it come from and from where does it derive its right to speak? How could it be legitimated? . . . if you claim that you are opening up a radical interrogation, if you wish to place your discourse at the level at which we place ourselves, you know very well that it will enter our game, and, in turn, extend the very dimension that it is trying to free itself from.[27]

In answer, Foucault confesses to a certain diffidence:

I admit that this question embarrasses me more than your earlier objections. I am not entirely surprised by it; but I would have preferred to leave it in suspense a little longer. This is because, for the moment, and as far ahead as I can see, my discourse, far from determining the locus in which it speaks, is avoiding the ground on which it could find support.[28]

And, in fact, Foucault never really does provide a satisfactory solution, at least not in his 'archaeological' phase. In his later 'genealogical' phase, he tries to claim that his own knowing and consciousness is really an act, or an abstract force on a level with all other abstract forces. But this claim will have to be examined later, in relation to the general philosophical position of Post-Structuralism.

Part Three

Post-Structuralist philosophy

Preliminaries

The dilemma that Foucault is coming up against at the end of *The Order of Things* and the end of *The Archaeology of Knowledge* is a problem that hangs over all the earlier Superstructuralists. It is easy enough for the theory of epistēmēs to encompass the thought of other historical periods; but when it encompasses the thought of our own present-day period, it also encompasses the thought of the thinker of the theory of epistēmēs. The power of received social discourse suddenly becomes an embarrassment when Foucault himself has to submit to its control. It is a classic case of a deterministic theory that reflexively determines itself out of existence.

Similarly with the Semioticians: the dilemma rears its head as soon as Semiotic analysis is applied not just to other people's societies but to our own. Lévi-Strauss can consider himself a Marxist whilst showing how primitive communities are ruled by an all-encompassing sign-field; he can look with favour upon the harmonious social integration of primitive communities as analogous to the harmonious social integration of a future Marxist community. But it is a different story when the Semioticians apply the concept of an all-encompassing sign-field to present-day society – to advertising, fashion, news reporting, etc. For now the principle of harmonious social integration works to the benefit of the existing capitalist and consumerist system which most Superstructuralists would want to condemn. Yet if the sign-field really is all-encompassing, their condemnation can have no ground to stand upon. The more power they attribute to signs and social meanings, the more they deprive themselves of the right to take up a position outside the capitalist and consumerist system, the more they deny themselves the right to reject it or envisage alternatives to it. Anti-establishment politics becomes an impossibility.

Post-Structuralism escapes from this dilemma, but not by making either of the two obvious appeals against an existing state of society. Post-Structuralism does not counter superficial social conformity by invoking deeper necessities of biological nature, nor does it counter external social imposition by invoking a free will that comes from within. To make either of these appeals would be to go back upon the whole logic of the Superstructuralist position, as developed by the Structuralists and the Semioticians, by Lacan and Althusser and Foucault. But Post-Structuralism does not go back upon the logic of the Superstructuralist position. Instead, it builds on top of the Superstructuralist position more superstructurally than ever; it carries the same logic even further in the same direction. With Post-Structuralism, the old paradoxes are not dismantled but redoubled.

What the Post-Structuralists invoke as an alternative is an even more sign-ish version of the Sign itself. Characteristically, they distinguish between two possible modes of functioning for the Sign. On the one hand, there is the conventional mode where the Sign works rigidly and despotically and predictably. This is the mode that Structuralists and Semioticians analyse. On the other hand, there is an unconventional mode where the Sign works creatively and anarchically and irresponsibly. This is the mode that represents the real being of the Sign. And when we are true to the real being of the Sign, we find that it subverts the socially controlled system of meaning, and, ultimately, socially controlled systems of every kind.

In Part Three, then, I shall be focusing upon a new philosophical priority: not a priority of the Sign over Objective Things and Subjective Mind, but a priority of the Anti-social Sign over the Social Sign. I shall be arguing that this priority is the common theme of all Post-Structuralists – of Derrida, Kristeva, the later Barthes, the 'genealogical' Foucault, Deleuze and Guattari, and Baudrillard. And I shall be trying to show how the Anti-Social Sign, in every case, possesses three essential qualities: it *moves*, it *multiplies* and it is *material*.

This last quality will require special attention. For it may well appear that, by making the Sign *material*, the Post-Structuralists have finally discarded all notion of objective ideas, and have finally cut off all connection with Metaphysical philosophy. But appearances are here deceptive. For, as we shall see, the Post-Structuralists make the Sign material only in a very unusual sense. And although they no longer have any use for the concept of all-encompassing systems of binary opposition or for the concept of objective ideas socially embedded in laws and customs and institutions, yet there are other concepts in Metaphysical philosophy upon which they draw more strongly than ever.

10

Derrida and language
as Writing

(i)

The key field for the development of Post-Structuralism is, once
again, the key Superstructuralist field of language theory. And
the key figure in this development is Jacques Derrida. (Gillès
Deleuze was advancing towards a Post-Structuralist position at
approximately the same time as Derrida, but Deleuze achieved
an impact only after Derrida had first cleared the way.) It is
Derrida's three crucial books of 1967 that mark the arrival of
Post-Structuralism: *Writing and Difference*, *Speech and Phenomena*
and *Of Grammatology*.

Derrida builds his Post-Structuralist theory of language upon
the destruction of Edmund Husserl's phenomenological theory
of language. Husserl is in search of an especially 'true' level of
language – from an 'I'-philosopher's point of view. For Husserl,
'true' language is necessarily and exclusively human, and he
draws an absolute distinction between human signs and natural
signs. This leads him to regard as incidental to linguistic
meaning the associations that words may cause to form in the
mind of a receiver – since such associations may also form in the
mind in relation to natural non-verbal phenomena (thus visible
smoke makes us think of invisible fire, etc.). Husserl sees 'true'
language in terms of 'expression', where 'expression' is meaning
as willed and intended by an utterer. 'Expression' exists only to

the extent that some individual mind is actually thinking it at the moment of utterance. As Derrida puts it on Husserl's behalf, 'expression . . . is meant, conscious through and through, and intentional'.[1] Meaning thus understood is not just meaning in the sense that *words mean*, but in the sense that *someone means them to mean*. In the ordinary way, we think of the physical signifier as inhabited and animated by the content of a signified; but Husserl goes beyond this, and insists that the signified itself must be inhabited and animated by an act of consciousness, a wanting-to-say, a 'vouloir-dire'.

This orientation towards 'expression' tilts Husserl's theory of language inevitably towards the use of Voice. In person-to-person speech, the speaker is standing directly in front of the hearer, who can more readily imagine and locate the required act of animating consciousness. In such a situation, the meaning may well seem to be controlled behind the words, especially if the speaker imposes an authoritative interpretation: 'No, what I meant was . . .', 'No, what I was trying to say was . . .'. It is as though the very airiness of words on the breath, the very transparency of the medium in which spoken signifiers so briefly live, actually allowed the hearer to look straight through into the speaker's mind.

But even this is not in the end enough for Husserl. After all, what could have caused the idea that anyone else has a mind in the first place, if not their words, their signifiers? Husserl's difficulties over the problem of intersubjectivity are notorious. And in his search for an especially 'true' level of language, he eventually relegates even person-to-person speech to a secondary status, and discovers 'expression' most purely present in the *intra*-subjective use of Voice, in interior monologue. In the heavenly state of interior monologue, the spirit of what one wants to say is no longer clogged and trammelled by the physical integument of an external signifier, which more worldly forms of communication require. When one talks to oneself, or when one talks to others and hears oneself speak ('s'entendre parler'), one understands perfectly and directly the intention that animates the words. The inward Voice puts the utterance and its reception right up against each other, absolutely adjacent within a single consciousness; no medium, not even an interval of air, divides them. As Derrida once again describes it on Husserl's behalf, 'My words are "alive" because they seem not to leave me: not to fall outside me, outside my breath, at a visible distance; not to cease to belong to me, to be at my disposition "without further props".'[2] The inward Voice takes place in time but it does not take place in space.

But by this stage, something very strange has happened. For, as Husserl admits, his conception of interior monologue requires that one already knows everything one is going to say to oneself even before starting to say it. Meaning is already shared between the uttering and receiving halves of the mind even before being formulated into words. In effect, language has been reduced to a mere appendage, and has no real reason for continuing to exist at all. Husserl's insistence that 'true' language is necessarily and exclusively human has enabled him to dissolve the existence of objective verbal signs entirely in favour of subjective human ideas. This is perhaps a satisfactory conclusion from the viewpoint of an 'I'-philosopher, but it is a highly unsatisfactory conclusion from the viewpoint of anyone who wants to consider language as an important reality in its own right.

Derrida, who wants to do just that, therefore reverses the entire chain of Husserl's argument. For Derrida, 'true' language is not language at its most human but language at its most language-y, language at its most self-sufficient – even to the extent of being independent of human beings. Derrida insists upon 'the structure peculiar to language alone, which allows it to function entirely *by itself* when its intention is cut off from intuition'.[3] So whereas Husserl tilts all language towards interior monologue as the extreme case of Voice, Derrida tilts all language towards the opposite extreme of Writing.

Writing is language at its most self-sufficient because it is language at its most spatial. Writing exists, not insubstantially in the mind, nor briefly and transparently in sound-waves of the air, but solidly and enduringly in marks upon a page. And such marks do not need to be propped up by the presence of their maker; on the contrary, their maker is always essentially absent, and may even be dead:

For the written to be the written, it must continue to 'act' and to be legible even if what is called the author of the writing no longer answers for what he has written . . . whether he is provisionally absent, or if he is dead, or if in general he does not support, with his absolutely current and present intention or attention, the plenitude of his meaning.[4]

Writing is 'orphaned, and separated at birth from the assistance of its father'.[5] From the reader's side of things, the very physicality of Writing stands in the way of any direct communication of intention.

A similar situation also appears on the writer's side of things. Writing for the writer serves to place concepts on reserve, to postpone them, to put them outside of consciousness until called for. Since the invention of Writing, human beings have not needed to keep concepts mentally present, held up before the mind's inward eye. In its function as an *aide-mémoire*, Writing represents the passage of thought *out of consciousness*. In Derrida's words, 'Writing, a mnemotechnic means, supplanting good memory, spontaneous memory, signifies forgetfulness . . . its violence befalls the soul as unconsciousness.'[6] The moment-by-moment stream of subjective ideas, the very quick of phenomenological life, dies away into the solid inanimate marks of Writing on the page.

Still, the obvious question remains: how can Derrida justify the priority of Writing in a theory of language? One might justify the priority of Voice by arguing that speech at least comes first in the history of the human race, and first in the development of every growing child. But Writing, by the same argument, looks irredeemably secondary, a mere superstructure added on top of the basic oral form. In order to justify the priority of Writing, Derrida has to turn the common-sense way of looking at the world completely upside-down.

One of the arguments against Writing is disposed of easily enough however: the argument that the marks on the page merely stand for the sounds of spoken language. This is valid for languages which have phonetic scripts, where the letter 'h' merely stands for the spoken 'h' sound, and so on. But as Derrida points out, it is not valid for languages such as Chinese and Egyptian, which have hieroglyphic and ideogrammatic scripts. In such scripts, the written sign does not need to go by way of a spoken sign to do its signifying. And, historically, the development of hieroglyphic and ideogrammatic scripts precedes the development of phonetic scripts. When Derrida thinks of Writing as an especially 'true' level of language, he is thinking above all of ideograms and rebuses.

However, it still cannot be denied that, in the history of the human race as in the development of every growing child, the use of speech comes before the use of writing. Nor does Derrida deny it. Rather he denies an assumption that we ordinarily make without even thinking about it: the assumption that the original form of a thing is somehow also its 'truest' form. Thus we tend to assume that we could finally explain language if only we could rediscover its most rudimentary beginnings in primitive communication. Such an assumption comes very naturally to us, but we would be hard pressed to justify it on rational grounds. So Derrida proposes instead a radical separation of historical and conceptual priority. (This is also Spinoza's move, when he attributes primary reality to that which can be thought independently, that which can be thought without thinking of anything else.) Derrida recognizes that the *fact* of writing follows from the *fact* of speech, but he none the less asserts that the *idea* of speech depends upon the *idea* of writing. Or to put it another way, writing is the logically fundamental condition to which language has always aspired.

No doubt this is a difficult position to grasp. But consider an analogy: the case of a growing tree. Ordinarily we tend to imagine – even when we know better – that a tree rises and flourishes by virtue of some deep and inwardly hidden source of life. We tend to imagine some single essential centre which was there in the earliest stages of growth, and which has remained constant under all later increments. But in fact, of course, a tree lives on the outside, by the circulation which flows through its green bark and sapwood; and its centre is mere dead heartwood, endlessly supplanted and left behind.

Or consider another analogy, somewhat closer to home: the history of the 'language' of mathematics. We might expect to arrive at the 'truest' form of mathematics by tracing all later developments back to the most rudimentary origins – back to actual counting operations with sticks or stones or beads or whatever. But such actual operations in the real world have been curiously supplanted and left behind in modern mathematics. Most famously, the square root of minus one does not exist in real-world terms at all. In order to allow for the viability of concepts such as the square root of minus one, modern philosophers of mathematics have had to propose an idea of mathematics as a kind of play or game, where rules are made up and followed through to their conclusions regardless of any applicability in the real world. The idea of actual counting operations appears as only a secondary and as it were accidental offshoot of this logically fundamental idea of mathematics as a whole. In a sense, mathematics reveals its 'truest' form in its latest, most 'unnatural', most supplementary developments. (Characteristically, Husserl saw a crisis of mathematical symbolism in the fact that symbols were being manipulated without any animating intention-to-signify.)[7]

Derrida generalizes this kind of situation into a new centrifugalist way of looking at the world. Against the orthodox logic of origins he pits an unorthodox logic of supplements, where what's added on later is always liable to predominate over what was there in the first place. 'The strange structure of the supplement appears ... by delayed reaction, a possibility produces that to which it is said to be added on.'[8] And in fact, this unorthodox logic is to some extent present in all Superstructuralism. For, as we have seen, the Superstructuralist vision of superstructures is precisely a recognition that a culture which is added on later can predominate over a nature which was there in the first place. In the Superstructuralist vision of superstructures, culture has become so fundamental to human existence that there is now no possibility of delving down under it. In this respect, the Superstructuralists even before Derrida already make a separation between historical and conceptual priority.

But the Superstructuralists before Derrida stop short. Although they reject nature for culture, they still allow an ideal of what's 'natural' to influence their conception of culture – and especially their conception of language. Thus Saussure praises speech as the earliest and 'truest' level of language, and inveighs against previous linguists who have supposedly distorted their study of language by paying too great an attention to 'unnatural' writing. As for Lévi-Strauss, he values this earliest and 'truest' level of language for its role in bonding together the earliest and 'truest' form of society. Like his mentor, Rousseau, he hankers nostalgically after the organic unity of the primitive community, 'a community immediately present to itself, without difference, a community of speech where all the members are within earshot'.[9] Consequently he sees the advent of writing as a fall from grace, and he bemoans in modern literate society the disintegration, dehumanization and disappearance of collective responsibility which supposedly follow from a lack of direct person-to-person communication. In this respect, Lévi-Strauss's anthropology is centripetalist.

Here we come to a parting of paths between the earlier Superstructuralists and the Post-Structuralists. Derrida goes all the way with the separation between historical and conceptual priority. He overturns our assumptions about origins in culture no less than our assumptions about origins in nature. For Derrida, the logic of supplements also applies to our way of thinking about language itself; and, as we shall presently see, also applies to our way of thinking about meaning within language.

(ii)

When Derrida reverses the entire chain of Husserl's argument, he embraces a condition of language that Husserl regarded as unthinkable. For Husserl insisted upon the mental meaning behind the verbal meaning in order to keep verbal meaning under control. The utterer's mind is the place where one can locate a single essential centre of meaning which was there in the beginning and which remains constant under all later increments and associations. The utterer's mind is the place where one can locate an ideal definitive gold standard of meaning that all subsequent readings must aspire to approach. When Husserl subjects verbal meaning to mental meaning, he subjects it to a principle of mastery and authority.

Derrida, on the other hand, discards this principle completely. What's in the writer's mind has no special priority over the meaning of his words. On the contrary, the writer only discovers the meaning of his words in the act of writing them. As Derrida, on behalf of all writers, confesses, 'before me, the signifier on its own says more than I believe that I meant to say, and in relation to it, my meaning-to-say is submissive rather than active'.[10] The written sign is not *sent* but only *received*; even the writer is just another reader.

The practical consequences for language are demonstrated when Derrida 'reads' particular words in the texts of other philosophers. Thus in Rousseau's *Essay on the Origin of Languages* he seizes upon the word 'supplément'.[11] Rousseau is trying to dismiss writing as merely superfluous and added-on, as supplementary in a damning sense. But in language at large, the word carries a further sense, and Derrida quotes the *Littré* definition of 'suppléer': ' "1. To add what is missing, to supply a necessary surplus." '[12] From this it becomes clear that the supplement is added on only because of a lack in the original, and hence is not really superfluous at all. The word itself, according to Derrida, will not abide by the single essential centre that Rousseau wished to give it.

Similarly with the Greek word 'pharmakon', which can mean both 'poison' and 'remedy'. When Plato, in the *Phaedrus*, applies the word to writing, he seems to be condemning writing as a 'poison' (at least in the standard French translations). But Derrida opens the word up to its other sense of 'remedy', claiming that 'the word *pharmakon* is caught in a chain of significations . . . [which] is not, simply, that of the intentions of an author who goes by the name of Plato'.[13] According to Derrida, the Greek language is saying through Plato's text two quite divergent things about writing, simultaneously and undecidably.

What's more, Derrida's reading of 'pharmakon' extends into even more remote and derivative meanings. Thus the 'pharmakon' as a drug in liquid form further implies dye and colouring and perfume; dye and colouring and perfume further imply the cosmetics used by actors; and the cosmetics used by actors further imply the festivals during which plays (in Greek times) were performed.[14] Or, on another tack, the 'pharmakon' further implies the etymologically related word 'pharmakos', meaning 'sorceror'; and (because sorcerors were expelled from the cities) 'pharmakos' further implies a scapegoat or sacrifice given up for the good of the community. The centrifugal movement of meaning within language could hardly be more plainly demonstrated.

Derrida's method of reading is obviously very similar to the method of reading developed, prior to any Superstructuralist influence, by modern Anglo-Saxon literary critics. Nor is this similarity surprising. For, in dealing with literature, the critic confronts the problem of the writer's absence in peculiarly acute form: not only is the writer liable to be dead and several centuries removed, but his or her meaning is liable to be quite disconnected from the facts of his or her life, even in an apparently autobiographical poem. What's more, the literary value of a poem does not seem to depend upon any real communicative function: it makes no difference to the value of a poem if it should turn out to have been produced by a chimpanzee randomly hitting the keys of a typewriter. Hence the general acceptance of Wimsatt's 'Intentional Fallacy', and the widespread critical view that the meanings of poems come from words and not from minds. And hence the concurrent discovery of a new method of reading literature, which no longer assumes that a poem has a single essential centre upon which meaning ought to converge, or even upon which the interpretations of different critics ought to converge. Like Derrida, modern Anglo-Saxon literary critics see meaning spreading out amongst undecidable ambiguities (as witness Empson's *Seven Types of Ambiguity*) or existing in divergent states of paradox and tension (as witness Cleanth Brooks's *The Well Wrought Urn* and Allen Tate's *On the Limits of Poetry*). Like Derrida (and like Nietzsche), modern Anglo-Saxon literary critics have no use for the Apollonian virtues of diaphanousness and univocity.[15]

However, Derrida's method of reading is more extreme than that of the Anglo-Saxon literary critics. And the theory behind his method is even more extreme than the method itself. For, according to Derrida, the centrifugal movement of any single word ultimately spreads out across every other word in the whole language. As he puts it:

> Like any text, the text of 'Plato' couldn't not be involved, at least in a virtual, dynamic, lateral manner, with all the words that composed the system of the Greek language. Certain forces of association unite . . . the words 'actually present' in a discourse with all the other words in the lexical system, whether or not they appear as 'words'.[16]

That Derrida does not actually carry his reading of the 'phar-makon' thus far is due to practical, not theoretical, limitations.

In fact, there is an important philosophical difference be-tween Derrida and the Anglo-Saxon literary critics. For when the critics multiply meanings, those meanings are still con-ceived in the ordinary way as mental contents and images – and modern Anglo-Saxon literary critics have a particular penchant for perceptual images. In effect, the critics treat written signs like natural signs. For natural signs do not exist in the mind of an author, and they mean whatever anyone, in any context, can take them to mean. (Thus visible smoke can mean not only invisible fire but also undried wood, the presence of intruders, a northerly wind, a meal in preparation, cover and camouflage, etc., etc.) Yet the meanings of natural signs still exist in a mind: the mind of an interpreter, the mind of a reader. This typically Anglo-Saxon position is the position that Husserl was trying to oppose when he sought to draw an absolute distinction between human signs and natural signs.

But when Derrida in turn opposes Husserl, he arrives at a more radical philosophical position altogether. For Derrida refuses to allow meanings in any mind at all. He conceives of meaning in a new and extraordinary way that involves no movement from marks on the page to mental contents and images. And he gives a very simple answer to the old philo-sophical problem of the elusive signified – the problem that, when we try to look at the meaning of a word in our minds, we never seem to encounter any decisive mental content or image but only absence and emptiness. Derrida's answer is that the signified does not exist. The signified, so far as Derrida is concerned, is merely an illusion that human beings have in-vented because they have feared to face up to the consequences of a materialist conception of language.

Derrida thus carries to its logical conclusion the general Superstructuralist tendency – initiated by Saussure and de-veloped by Benveniste – to favour the signifier at the expense of the signified. But in Derrida's theory of language, these sig-nifiers are not like the old signifiers, mere inert physical marks on the page, mere things in the world of things. These signifiers are above all *signifying*, that is, pointing away from themselves, pointing away to other signifiers. Although Derrida's theory of language involves no movement from signifier to signified, it still involves movement – from signifier to signifier. In effect, signifying is nothing more or less than signifiers *in motion*. Such is the new and extraordinary way in which Derrida conceives of meaning. Writing exists only in terms of spatially independent signifiers, but spatially independent signifiers exist only in terms of a spatially independent movement running through them.

What's more, this movement is unstoppable. In the ordinary conception of meaning, the signifier points away from itself but the signified does not. As idea or as image in the reader's mind, the signified represents a terminus where meaning comes to a halt. But in Derrida's conception, one signifier points away to another signifier, which in turn points away to another signifier, which in turn points away to another signifier, and so on *ad infinitum*. As Derrida puts it:

> The meaning of meaning ... is infinite implication, the indefinite referral of signifier to signifier ... its force is a certain pure and infinite equivocality which gives signified meaning no respite, no rest, but engages it in its own *economy* so that it always signifies again and differs.[17]

There is no escape from the movement of signifiers signifying; there is only an interminable pushing off and toppling forward and pushing off again.

Derrida describes this state of language as a state of *dissemination*. Here is no full rich harvest of signified meanings such as modern Anglo-Saxon literary critics delight to find, but rather a kind of endless loss and spillage: 'seed scattered wastefully outside'.[18] *Dissemination* must be distinguished from *univocity* or the state of single meanings maintained by the signified in the writer's mind; but it must also be distinguished from *polysemy* or the state of multiple meanings maintained by the signified in the reader's mind. *Dissemination* is the state of perpetually unfulfilled meaning that exists in the absence of all signifieds.

By removing the signified, Derrida thus removes the last human control over language. In the absence of all signifieds, language takes on its own kind of energy and creativity, quite distinct from any subjective energy or creativity on the part of individual writers or readers. This is an energy and creativity to which individual writers and readers can only *abandon* themselves. In *dissemination*, language manages to avoid both *social responsibility* and *individual irresponsibility*: 'responsibility and individuality are values that no longer predominate here: that is the first effect of dissemination'.[19] In *dissemination*, language reveals an anarchic and unpredictable level of functioning, subversive of all rigid proper meanings on the ordinary socially controlled level. Such is the Post-Structuralist mode of language, the mode of the Sign's real being.

(iii)

Language in the mode of *dissemination* is far beyond anything to be found in the theories of Saussure or Benveniste or Jakobson. Yet these earlier linguists prepared the ground for Derrida by depriving words of their ordinary substantial centres, their simple positive phonetic and semantic contents. For without such contents, words are no longer weighted down and anchored, can no longer stand still and stable by themselves. There is a potential for centrifugalism even in the theories of these earlier linguists.

But Saussure and company have a way of defeating centrifugalism. Although a word cannot stand still and stable by itself, it can stand still and stable by leaning up against other words. Its centrifugal tendencies can be halted at the boundaries (whether hierarchically organized in Jakobson's model or all-on-a-level in Saussure's model) which differentiate it from other words. By differentiation, all words together stand still and stable in a total simultaneous system. *Simultaneous*, in that the system only balances if words push against each other at exactly the same time; *total*, in that the system only balances if there are no internal gaps to give words room for falling, and no surrounding void to give words room for dispersing. For a state of perfect equilibrium, words need to be packed tightly up together within a closed space.

The concept of a total simultaneous system thus recovers what might have been lost: the traditional view that a word is always self-identical in sound and meaning, always fixed in the same place. But, as we have already seen, this concept brings grave problems in its wake. Thus the system – which is the system of 'langue' – necessarily precedes any particular usage of words in 'parole'; yet, as Derrida remarks, it is hard to believe that 'langue' has 'simply fallen from the sky ready made'.[20] A first problem for Structural Linguists is that they cannot explain how 'langue' might be generated by way of 'parole'. A second problem stems from a double action of the condition of totality. On the one hand, the condition of totality allows words no freedom or creativity or room for manoeuvre within the system; on the other hand, any knowledge of the system must necessarily be a knowledge of the totality, a particularly lofty and all-encompassing knowledge. But such lofty and all-encompassing knowledge is incompatible with the fact that the knower also belongs within the system, and can only know in terms of the words of the system. The nature of the system (as a totality) militates against any knowledge of the system (as a totality). As we have seen, this problem comes to a head in Structuralist Semiotics and Foucault's epistemic history.

Derrida can afford to dispense with the concept of a total simultaneous system because he no longer seeks to preserve the traditional view that a word is always self-identical and fixed in the same place. He has no use for '[differences] inscribed once and for all in a closed system, a static structure that a synchronic and taxonomic operation could exhaust'.[21] Language in the mode of dissemination is endlessly unbalanced and out of equilibrium. No longer do words push against one another at the same time; they push successively, in causal chains, toppling one another over like lines of falling dominoes. Or, to coin an electrical metaphor: whereas Saussurean 'langue' exists merely in terms of static voltage differentials between positive and negative poles, language as dissemination exists in terms of currents that flow from pole to pole (to pole to pole), creating and uncreating voltage differentials. The Structuralist kind of analysis is 'possible only after a certain defeat of force'; it sees force only on the level of its effects, only on the level of 'the accomplished, the constituted, the *constructed*'.[22] '*Form* fascinates,' says Derrida, 'when one no longer has the force to understand force from within itself.'[23] When Derrida understands force from within itself, he reopens the dimension of time that the Structuralists excluded from their spatial models, the dimension of time where force can actually *act*.

Derrida's theory of language still works by differentiation – but a differentiation with a difference. Or, to be more precise, with a 'différance'. This specially invented term makes manifest the two meanings of the French verb 'différer'. As Derrida describes it, 'On the one hand, [différer] indicates difference as distinction, inequality, or discernibility; on the other, it expresses the interposition of delay, the interval of a *spacing* and *temporalizing* that puts off until "later" what is presently denied.'[24] In this latter sense, 'différer' approximates to the sense of the English verb 'to defer'; and, like the English verb, brings into play the notion of an action *in time*. Differentiated by 'différance', the meanings of 'pharmakon' no longer compose a static simultaneous opposition: the meaning 'poison' does not exist merely by virtue of its *difference* from the meaning 'remedy', but also by virtue of its *deferring* of the meaning 'remedy'. And the meaning that is deferred is put off only *for the present*; it still impends, it still awaits, and *in time* the meaning that defers will have to flow over into it.

The sense of deferring goes beyond the sense of difference in another way too. In a static simultaneous opposition, the alternative meanings of 'pharmakon' simply exclude one another; but when one meaning defers and flows over into another, there is evidently a kind of sameness involved. Derrida describes the new situation with the aid of a somewhat paradoxical distinction between sameness and identity: '*différance* is . . . the element of the *same* (to be distinguished from the identical) in which these [static simultaneous] oppositions are announced'.[25] Or, in another description, 'The *same*, which is not the identical . . . is precisely [différance], as the diverted and equivocal passage from one difference to another, one term of the opposition to the other.'[26] In 'différance', alternative meanings are not the same to the extent of being identified in a single meaning; they are the same to the extent that a single force passes through them, crosses the boundary between them.

Another boundary crossed is the boundary between 'parole' and 'langue'. In 'différance', an uttered word (such as 'pharmakon') exists by its deferring of unuttered words (such as 'pharmakos'). So when this deferring is allowed to flow, a single force passes from words in a present state to words in an absent state, from Plato in particular to the Greek language in general, from 'parole' to 'langue'. Derrida's theory of language can actually generate 'langue' out of 'parole'.

Derrida's theory of language thus goes beyond the earlier Structuralist theory in many ways. But it is not without ancestry in Metaphysical philosophy – and particularly in the philosophy of Hegel. Derrida himself observes with approval certain passages translated by Koyré from Hegel's Jena *Logic*, where 'the term "different" is taken here in an active sense'.[27] In fact, Hegel's philosophical system is dynamic and creative, a successive, self-producing chain of concepts. The differences between Being and Nothing, or the One and the Many, or Repulsion and Attraction, can be taken in a static sense – and I took them thus when comparing the binarism of Structuralists to the binarism of Metaphysical philosophy at the end of Section (ii) in Chapter 7 above. For Hegel, however, such static differences are really only the effects of a deeper activity. The concept of Being, for instance, is not just *different* from the concept of Nothing; it *defers* the concept of Nothing. Thus Being, as Hegel thinks it, is pure contentless 'is'-ness, in the sense that a thing simply *is*, but *is not* green or soft or a ball or anything in particular. But to think Being in such a way is to think a thing that is nothing – and thereby to arrive at the concept of Nothing. For Hegel, the concept of Being temporarily puts off the concept of Nothing, then eventually flows over into it. Similarly with all the other oppositions, where the first term turns out to be unstable and unbalanced and in need of the second term. Hegel is perpetually crossing boundaries between apparently incompatible concepts. Like Derrida, he works with a logic of sameness *and* difference that quite outleaps the ordinary logic of contradiction, the ordinary logic of identity *or* exclusion. Indeed, he explicitly condemns ordinary logic as a lower and limited form of reason.

However, this unbalancing movement still does not have the final say in Hegel's logic. For the movement from first term to second term is only a part of the Hegelian triad; there is also another, very different, movement that goes back over both terms and raises them up into the higher unity of a third term. Thus the passage of Being into Nothing (and, contrariwise, of Nothing into Being) is comprehended in the concept of Becoming (i.e. the concept of change as a coming into or going out of existence). By this other movement, Hegel manages to accumulate his terms as he goes along, until the final synthesizing concept of the Absolute Idea effectively comprehends absolutely everything that has gone before. In this way, Hegel's system is a *total* system even though it is not a *simultaneous* system. For all its dynamic instability, it reaches in the end a closed and completed state, just like the Saussurean system of 'langue'.

The movement to a third term has no place in Derrida's theory of language. In Derrida's theory, oppositions are unbalanced '*without ever* constituting a third term, without ever leaving room for a solution in the form of speculative dialectics'.[28] For Derrida is dealing not with concepts but with signs, and with signs whose signifying appears in mechanical rather than mental form, as a mere motion running through signifiers. And clearly, a mere mechanical motion can never rise up and *comprehend* in the way that ideas can. To think in terms of mechanical motion is to think in terms of spillage rather than accumulation, openendedness rather than totality. It is to abandon the security of an investment where the stakes are always conserved for the risk of a game where every throw is a winning and a losing, a losing and a winning. Such is the difference between Hegel's 'restricted economy' and Derrida's 'general economy'.[29] Derrida follows the Hegelian path to irrationalist consequences that Hegel himself drew back from. Where Hegel envisaged a logic beyond ordinary logic, Derrida envisages a logic beyond any form of reason whatsoever.

11

Derrida's general theory
of Writing

(i)

For Derrida, as for all Superstructuralists, language constitutes the human world and the human world constitutes the whole world. So, by the same progression that leads from Saussurean linguistics to general Semiotics, Derrida expands his theory of language into a philosophy of the world *as* language. Only now, of course, language and world are to be conceived in terms of Writing rather than in terms of 'langue'. When Derrida displaces objective things and subjective ideas from their traditional priority, it is Writing that he puts ahead of them.

This is still a monism, but its emphasis falls somewhat differently to the monism of the Structuralists and Semioticians. For when 'langue' is put ahead of objective things and subjective ideas, it has the effect of sending ideas out into the outside world: the 'glamour' of wine supplants the reality of wine, the category of 'rape' supplants the reality of rape, and so on. But when Writing is put ahead of objective things and subjective ideas, it has the effect of bringing a kind of thing-ish-ness into the inside world. It materializes subjectivity.

So, when Derrida opposes traditional philosophical dualism, he particularly opposes the mind-soul-spirit term of that dualism. Indeed, he does not see mind simply balanced against matter, or soul simply balanced against body, or spirit simply balanced against natural world; he sees a profound inequality behind these apparent polarizations. For, according to Derrida, mind and soul and spirit assume a very definite moral superiority over their 'lower', 'merely physical', counterparts. In what is traditionally regarded as the proper, rational, ordered state of dualism, the mind comprehends matter, the soul rules the body, and the spirit makes laws in the natural world. As Derrida puts it, 'In a classical philosophical opposition we are not dealing with the peaceful coexistence of a *vis-à-vis* but rather with a violent hierarchy. One of the two terms governs the other . . . or has the upper hand.'[1] The mind-soul-spirit term is dominant, and, as such, bears the prime responsibility for keeping the whole dualism in place.

Derrida thus wields his concept of Writing against the mind-soul-spirit term. In effect, he argues that the unconscious mind underlies the conscious mind, and that the unconscious mind exists in the form of Writing. This is Writing as 'arche-writing', a fundamental script or hieroglyphics written upon the matter of the brain. Such a script precedes all writing-upon-a-page, and, for that matter, also precedes all speech – even in the history of the human race or the development of the growing child.

Derrida derives his theory of 'arche-writing' from Freud, and especially from Freud's essay 'Note on the Mystic Writing Pad'. In this essay, Freud compares the psychic apparatus to the Mystic (or Magic) Writing Pad, still sold as a novelty toy for children. The pad is made up of a transparent sheet of celluloid on top of a sheet of greaseproof-like paper on top of a waxed base. A stylus pressing down upon the celluloid presses the paper down against the waxed base, and this latter contact causes the darkness of the base to show through as writing on the lighter-coloured paper. Such writing is not actually deposited on the paper, and can be made to disappear simply by lifting the paper away from the base. However, as Freud points out, the waxed base itself still presumably retains the mark inscribed by the stylus even when the writing is no longer legible. In this respect, the base can be compared to the unconscious mind, which retains what it does not perceive, and the paper (and celluloid) can be compared to the perception-consciousness system, which transmits what it does not retain.

Derrida makes the most of this analogy when he interprets the role of *Bahnung* ('facilitation') and *Spur* ('the trace') in Freud's general model for perception and memory. In Freud's general model, a force excited in the individual's perceptual circuits passes through the neurological system of the brain, opening up or facilitating a pathway or trace of lowered electro-chemical resistance. This pathway or trace then remains as the physical form of an unconscious memory, the incised channel along which future forces may more easily flow and follow. Derrida accepts this theory of the trace, and ties it in with the writing inscribed upon the waxed base of the Mystic (or Magic) Writing Pad. For such writing also has the form of an incised channel, hollowed out by the pressure of the stylus. In Derrida's interpretation, the trace is therefore a sign, as writing is a sign.

What's especially important from Derrida's point of view is that the concept of the sign is hereby combined with the concept of causal force. Freud's general model for perception and memory is a *mechanical* model, where the passage of stimulus from perception to memory occurs in a purely physical way. And when Derrida turns the trace into a sign, he still leaves out all notion of mind or soul or spirit. For Derrida, the Mystic (or Magic) Writing Pad is a writing-*machine*, where the passage of pressure from stylus to waxed base occurs in a purely physical way. The legible appearance of the writing is relatively inciden-tal to the operation which inscribes the trace – and even more incidental when Derrida further supposes an accompanying operation which perpetually lifts the paper away from the base and perpetually erases the legible appearance of the writing.[2]

In fact, even in so far as the writing *does* appear on the surface of the Mystic (or Magic) Writing Pad, it is not by virtue of any contact between the paper (or celluloid) and the outside force of the stylus, but by virtue of a contact between the paper and the waxed base underneath it. The legible appearance of the writ-ing comes not from the stylus pressing *down*, but from the darkness of the base showing *up*. Or in other words, the legible appearance of the writing is produced indirectly, retrospec-tively, on the backstroke. Similarly in the case of the psychic apparatus. 'Writing,' says Derrida, 'supplements perception before perception even appears to itself.'[3]

Derrida here draws upon Freud's concept of *Nachträglichkeit*, the delayed effect, the experience which only surfaces to consciousness long after the actual event. For Derrida, the case of the delayed effect represents the fundamental case of all experience. For Derrida, even our most seemingly immediate experience is not a direct reflection of the outside world but a contact made with what has already been inscribed, unconsciously, in the memory. Even our perceptual images and impressions are no more than the kind of perceptual images and impressions that we get from reading a book. Perception is forever divided from the presence of 'the things themselves'. As Derrida, following his own interpretation of Peirce, puts it: 'the so-called "thing itself" is always already a *representamen* shielded from the simplicity of intuitive evidence'.[4] And, as with presence, so with the temporal present. We can never catch up with the actual moment of our sensory contact with the outside world, we are eternal latecomers to the 'now' of our own experience. 'The "perceived",' says Derrida, 'may be read only in the past, beneath perception and after it.'[5] The phenomenological concept of the absolute present moment, along with the phenomenological concept of 'the things themselves', is deconstructed as an illusion in Derrida's general theory of Writing.

This is a very strange condition to find ourselves in. Life becomes a kind of dream, as for the sleepers in Plato's cave. Indeed, our ordinary sleeping dreams – which give perhaps as close a glimpse of the unconscious mind as we can ever attain – also give perhaps as close a glimpse of this strange condition as we can ever attain. For in our dreams we often realize that someone has done something or said something even though we have never actually seen the doing or heard the saying. Or we seem to possess 'memories' which have never been acquired through present experience in the dream, and which can never be remembered in images of present experience. Such 'memories' fit well with Derrida's description of 'a "past" that has never been nor ever will be present'.[6] The time of a dream must thus be thought of according to what Derrida envisages as 'a different structure, a different stratification of time'.[7] Not only do we experience our dreams essentially through interpretations, we also experience them to a considerable extent in terms of after-effects.*

Of course, the idea that we live our lives in a kind of dream is liable to seem not only strange but also highly objectionable. We feel that such a condition reduces us to helplessness and insignificance. We feel dislodged from our proper position in the middle of our own experience, the position that the traditional model of the psychic apparatus allows us to claim. For, in the traditional model, excitations in the perceptual circuits must be cast upon the screen of consciousness as images and impressions and reflections of an outside world before passing through to be stored away (as implicit images and impressions and reflections of an outside world) in the memory. Consciousness thus takes command at the crucial point of experience, overlooking, mediating, taking in and giving out. With consciousness 'on top of' perception, we can justifiably feel a sense of mastery and control.

However, the traditional model runs into grave difficulties, both empirical and theoretical. Empirically, there is the difficulty of accounting for the fact of hypnotic recall. Under deep hypnosis, a patient can recover experiences which were repressed and kept out of consciousness at the time of their taking place, and, even more interestingly, can recover details of experiences which, though not exactly repressed, were not significant enough to be selected for presentation to consciousness at the time of their taking place. The facts of hypnotic recall indicate that the unconscious mind records a great deal more than consciousness has ever inspected; indeed, it has been suggested that the unconscious mind keeps a record in every finest detail of absolutely *everything*.

As for the theoretical difficulties of the traditional model, these have caused many a headache in the history of

---

* As regards the realization that someone has said something even though we have not actually heard the saying, it is especially interesting that in dreams we almost never listen to a speech or a conversation word for word. Derrida, interpreting Freud, makes the point that 'speech . . . figures in dreams much as captions do in comic strips'.[8] The point certainly tells against Husserl and his claims for Voice as the crucial form of language. At this depth of the unconscious mind, Voice hardly features at all.

philosophy. Where is the screen of consciousness to be located? How does it relate to the matter of the brain? How do we know that its images and impressions really are reflections of the outside world? These and similar difficulties have always beset philosophers who have tried to view the psychic apparatus as a kind of movie theatre, a non-stop picture show inside the head. Evidently a radical solution is called for; and Derrida provides a very radical solution indeed.

According to Derrida, consciousness (at least in the ordinary sense) is an illusion that human beings have invented because they have feared the consequences of a materialist conception of the brain. In this respect, the modern secular notion of mind is really no improvement upon older religious notions of soul and spirit. All such ghostly presences are in the same boat, along with that other ghostly presence already considered in the special theory of Writing – the ghostly presence of the signified. Indeed, Derrida regards mind as a signified that we attribute to the brain, Divine Spirit as a signified that we attribute to the natural world, and so on. In Derrida's terminology, all such ghostly presences are versions of 'logos' – a Greek word that illuminatingly brings together in a single concept the inward rational principle of verbal texts, the inward rational principle of human beings, and the inward rational principle of the natural universe. Even more illuminating, 'logos' combines all these meanings with a further meaning: 'the Law'. For 'logos' as an inward rational principle serves to control and take charge of outward material things. Any version of 'logos' can therefore give us the feeling of mastery and being 'on top'. And any version of 'logos' can save us from our greatest human fear of insecurity and 'letting go'. But any version of 'logos' is mere wishful thinking as far as Derrida is concerned.

(ii)

Derrida's general theory of Writing is thus a general theory of materialism. But materialism only in a very special sense. For when Derrida overturns our ordinary conception of mind in favour of a materialist conception of the brain, this is only by way of a first phase of overturning. In the second phase, our ordinary conception of matter has to be overturned too.[9] 'If I have not very often used the word "matter",' says Derrida, this is because the word 'has been too often reinvested with "logocentric" values, values associated with those of thing, reality, presence in general, sensible presence, for example, substantial plenitude, content, referent, etc.'[10] Needless to say, it is an extraordinary redefinition that can leave matter stripped clean of any suggestion of reality or referent or even *thing*.

In fact, it is *signifiers* that are fundamental in Derrida's general theory, just as in his special theory. And such signifiers are not to be conceived in the ordinary way: as things which *first* exist in their own right and *then* point away to some other thing. On the contrary, these signifiers signify *before* they are things; they point away from themselves even before they *are* themselves. 'The trace', says Derrida, 'must be thought before the entity.'[11] And 'the property of the representamen [i.e. signifier] is to be itself and another . . . to be separated from itself'.[12] Such is the highly paradoxical state of what Derrida calls 'radical alterity', and only in so far as we can think of matter in this state can we describe Derrida as a 'materialist': 'if, and in the extent to which, matter in this general economy designates . . . radical alterity . . . then what I write can be considered "materialist" '.[13]

This kind of materialism is clearly very different to the neurological positivists' kind of materialism. When neurological positivists study neurones and molecules and electrical charges in the brain, they are studying positive things and entities. The ultimate assumption behind such study is the old atomizing assumption that the scientist's key for unlocking all secrets is simply to observe entities on a sufficiently small scale. But in the meanwhile, the question as to how such entities might *signify* is conveniently left to one side.

Derrida, by contrast, is not concerned with entities in the brain but with the configurations between entities. He quotes with approval Freud's claim that 'thoughts and psychical structures in general must never be regarded as localized in organic elements of the nervous system but rather, as one might say, *between* them'.[14] And he insists that 'trace as memory is not a pure breaching [i.e. facilitation] that might be reappropriated at any time as simple presence; it is rather the ungraspable and invisible difference between breaches'.[15] In spite of his electrochemical terminology, Derrida has no real interest in the scientific study of that which is 'graspable' and 'visible' inside the brain.

But how do configurations signify? One possible way is the way of the computer. For, in a computer, electrical states signify not simply by what they *are*, but by a formal relation to what they *are not*. That is, the passage of a current signifies because it *is not* the absence of a current, and the absence of a current signifies because it *is not* the passage of a current. The flow of signifying through a computer cannot be studied as just a positive physical flow; it must be studied as a more-than-physical flow, taking in the negative as well as the positive.

However, the computer model will not in the end suffice for Derrida's purposes. For computers are designed to give *answers* to problems; and their flow of signifying is cashed in or redeemed when the human mind interprets a final output as the answer to an original input. In this respect, computers operate centripetally and require a return to origin. And in this respect, computers represent only a temporary postponement of the signified. But according to Derrida, what is postponed is never recovered and what is invested is never redeemed. According to Derrida, we must conceive of 'an expenditure without reserve' and 'an irreversible wearing-down of energy'.[16] Here is no cycling back to an origin, only a perpetual dispersal.

Another way in which configurations might signify is implicit in Derrida's terminology of channels, grooves, tracks, paths and furrows. In all such cases, the trace is not a simple self-sufficient thing, but an absence relative to something else. Thus we recognize a path as that which is taken away from the ordinary state of the forest, we recognize a track as that which is taken away from the ordinary state of the ground. And when we recognize such taking away, we also recognize that some past gouging force must have done the taking away. Thus the track points to the past passage of an animal, the path points to the past passage of a number of people. Channels, grooves, tracks, paths and furrows are all obvious natural signs, signifying away from themselves as soon as we look at them.

Unfortunately, though, the signifying of natural signs is not the kind of signifying that Derrida wants. For natural signs point only so far as some particular positive presence: to an animal, to a number of people, to the mental representation of an animal or a number of people. But Derrida's kind of signifying involves a more radical alterity altogether. 'Whoever believes that one tracks down some *thing*?' he asks. 'One tracks down tracks.'[17] Our ordinary way of thinking about tracks will not, in the end, suffice.

The difference can also be expressed in other terms. Our ordinary way of thinking about tracks is unsatisfactory because the movement by which the sign is read operates in the opposite direction to the movement by which the sign is written. That is, the sign is produced as the effect of a cause, and the reading of the sign reverses that causal sequence and deduces the cause from the effect. But this will not do for Derrida. For as long as we are still thinking in terms of two distinct movements, we are still caught in the trammels of traditional philosophical dualism. (Indeed, how can we think of an act of deduction if not as an act of *mind*?) Whereas Derrida insists upon closing the gap between writing and reading until 'constituted – written – meaning presents itself as prerequisitely and simultaneously *read*'.[18] And he explicitly claims that, in his general theory of Writing, 'meaning and force are united', and 'the distinction between force and meaning is derivative in relation to the archi-trace'.[19] Derrida is happy enough to think of the *writing* of the trace as equivalent to the causal production of a track; but he wants the reading of the trace to be a movement in the same direction, a further production – or implication – of more and more tracks.

What's needed, then, is an entirely new way of reading the trace. And we can see just such a way exemplified when Derrida reads the meaning of one particularly important path: the path carved out by the Nambikwara Indians. As described by Lévi-Strauss, this is a path cutting through the original natural forest of the Nambikwara territory; as discussed by Derrida, it is therefore a trace and a sign. But it is not a sign of its *cause*, it does not inspire a deduction about the passage of the people who made it. Instead, it inspires the following 'meditation':

One should meditate upon all of the following together: writing as the possibility of the road and of difference, the

history of writing and the history of the road, of the rupture, of
the *via rupta*, of the path that is broken, beaten, *fracta*, of the
space of reversibility and of repetition traced by the opening,
the divergence from, and the violent spacing, of nature, of the
natural, savage, salvage, forest.[20]

Such is the meaning of the path: a kind of expanding, unfolding,
general meaningfulness.

This is indeed a meditator's kind of meaning. It is not by
chance that Derrida so often speaks of 'meditating' and 'medi-
tations' in his writings. The mode of signifying with which we
are now dealing has much in common with the spiritual
exercise of meditation. It will cast considerable light upon
Derrida's theory of the trace if we analyse the analogy point by
point.

In the first place, meditation begins from a special type of
object or from a special type of word. If from an object, it is
typically a *shaped* object, a wave-hollowed pebble or whatever. If
from a word, it is typically a word without ordinary meaning
(such as the famous 'OM') or a word that loses its ordinary
meaning by being repeated over and over again. For the
purposes of meditation, natural object and human word are in
essentially the same condition. That is, they present themselves
as configurations, as patterns of formal difference. The object is
no longer a simple self-sufficient thing, but a sign; the word is
still a sign, but no longer expresses a humanly intended signified. The word is nothing more – and the object nothing less –
than a *signifier*. Which is precisely the condition that Derrida
attributes to the trace.

In the second place, this signifier without a signified does its
signifying in a very special direction. For the meditator, a
pebble or a word can generate meaning without ever referring to
any particular thing or inspiring any particular mental content.
For the meditator, meaning is an infinite implication that can
reach out to 'mean' the whole universe. This is the kind of
expanding, unfolding, general meaningfulness that we have
observed in the case of the Nambikwara path; and it is also the
kind of meaningfulness that we have observed in our earlier
examples of *dissemination*.

In the third place, meditation works by absence, by

negativity. For when the meditator concentrates upon a pebble or a word, this is not in order to fill the mind with it. On the contrary, the meditator concentrates upon a pebble or a word in order to empty the mind of all other contents. Meditation thus generates a sense of void, an infinity of space opening up on all sides. And it is into this emptiness that meaning spreads out – *sucked forth*, as it were, by the surrounding vacuum. Similarly in Derrida's theory of signifying. For Derrida proposes an absolute negativity that is no longer merely 'the reassuring *other* surface of the positive . . . it can no longer permit itself to be converted into positivity'.[21] In effect, a primordial self-deficiency underlies all positive entities. And it is this 'essential nothing on whose basis everything can appear and be produced within language'.[22] Here too, it seems possible to understand the movement of signifying as a kind of perpetual toppling outwards into empty space.

In the fourth place, meditation does not involve directed activity on the part of the subject. The meditator does not strive to grasp a meaning in the ordinary way; once the vacuum has been created, meaning spreads out all by itself. Hence the value of meditation as an antidote to the self-centred, goal-oriented ego. The meditator must learn how *not* to strive and grasp, must learn how to let go and open up the mind and surrender control. And here, once again, the principle of meditation is exactly analogous to the principle of signifying as Derrida understands it. For signifying as Derrida understands it is outside of the self, an objective and impersonal movement of meaning. To realize the real being of the Sign, one must learn how *not* to control and direct it, must learn how to leave it free to follow its own inclinations.

In all these many respects, then, the analogy with meditation helps us to form a model for the trace consistent with what Derrida requires. Signifying comes before the signifier, and nothing comes before signifying. Or, as we should perhaps more accurately express it, *Nothing* comes before signifying. For the movement of signifying is created by the *pull* of a vacuum, endlessly advancing and opening up ahead. No need, here, for the counter-causal act of deduction, the mental *push* involved in our ordinary way of thinking about channels, grooves, tracks, paths and furrows. Here, the movement of signifying goes forwards and onwards, implicating (though not producing) more and more tracks. And this movement, in its impersonality and its determinism, at least *resembles* the movement of causal force.

However, this movement cannot be located on the concrete plane where we usually locate the movement of causal force. For the vacuum here is not a real physical vacuum. How could spaces in the electro-chemical brain open up ahead *endlessly*? The vacuum here is an abstract vacuum, a vacuum of abstraction, which pulls away from the concrete plane altogether. The movement of signifying does not take place simply inside the brain – nor simply outside it either. The movement of signifying takes place in a realm where the distinction between inside and outside no longer has any relevance. We can, if we like, continue to follow Derrida by calling this realm the Unconscious. But we must recognize that Derrida's version of the Unconscious can no more be pinned down within separate human brains than within separate human minds. Freud, for one, would surely have had great difficulty in thinking this version of the Unconscious.

Clearly, we have reached a position far beyond any scientific conception of the universe. And Derrida himself proclaims the virtues of 'meta-rationality' and 'meta-scientificity'.[23] A strange position indeed: but not without a certain European ancestry. For elements of the same way of thinking appear in the Symbolist poets of the late nineteenth century, and also – once again – in the Metaphysical philosophers.

Like Derrida, the Symbolist poets had a vision of the world as writing. They particularly sought to 'read' this writing in the *natural* world, the natural world as composed of patterns, signs and configurations, all secretly implicating one another in interminable 'correspondences'. For the Symbolist poets, the natural world was *never less* than signifiers; but by the same token, their own writing was *never more* than signifiers. Hence the characteristic emphasis upon material properties of language in their own writing (as when Mallarmé lays out the words of 'Un Coup de Dès' as though the storm-tossed boat were tracing its motion directly on to the whiteness of the page). Like Derrida, the Symbolist poets show tendencies towards both mysticism and materialism, tendencies which appear contradictory, but which can none the less be understood in terms of a single coherent underlying position.*

As for the relation between Derrida and the Metaphysical philosophers, there are two especially relevant points of resemblance to consider. The first point has to do with the unusual importance that Metaphysical philosophers give to the principle of negativity. Spinoza starts the ball rolling with his claim that all determination is negation, i.e. what a thing *is* depends upon its limits, and these limits depend upon what the thing *is not*. Thus negativity can no longer be simply subordinated to positivity. Hegel carries this further with his claim that all negation is determination, i.e. what *is not* draws limits, and these limits determine what *is*. Positivity now can be actually subordinated to negativity. Hence the 'portentous power of the negative', as Hegel describes it, and hence the crucial role that negativity plays in undermining and unbalancing the successive terms in the Hegelian system. In fact, the principle of negativity is responsible for that dynamism of the Hegelian system which we observed at the end of Chapter 10. Derrida's only objection to Hegel's principle of negativity is that Hegel himself tries to draw back from its most radical consequences.[25]

The second point of resemblance emerges most strongly in relation to Spinoza. For Spinoza attempts to identify the force that runs through the mental world with the force that runs through the material world: 'the order and connection of ideas is the same as the order and connection of things' (*Ethics*, Part II, Proposition VII). This is essentially the same identification that Derrida attempts, when he attempts to unite causal force and meaning. And it depends upon the same double-sided divorce from our ordinary ways of thinking. For Spinoza's philosophy is on the one hand mystical, in the sense that it dissolves all ordinary thingishness and gives pride of place to bodiless abstract ideas. But on the other hand, it is also mechanical, in

---

* Particularly interesting in relation to Derrida is the curiously materialistic theory of the brain advanced by Rainer Maria Rilke. Fascinated by a similarity between the grooves in the coronal suture of the brain and the grooves in the wax cylinders that were played on early phonographs, this most mystical of Symbolist poets looked forward to the prospect of 'playing' the brain like a wax cylinder under some ultimate form of gramophone needle![24]

the sense that it discards the ordinary mental push of individual minds and allows ideas an objective impersonal deterministic movement of their own. On the one hand, a kind of mysticism: on the other hand, a kind of mechanism which seems to have its proper home in scientific materialism. The incongruity of the combination has often puzzled Spinoza's Anglo-Saxon commentators (Stuart Hampshire being perhaps the most recent example). But Derrida's position illuminates Spinoza's position. Spinoza is not a scientific materialist, but a materialist of a very different breed. Like Derrida, he is a Metaphysical materialist.

But although the position of the Metaphysical materialist is a coherent one, we do not have to accept that it is an all-encompassing one. Certainly, Derrida's kind of signifying is not simply causal force and not simply meaning; but it is also not what Derrida claims, the ultimate unification of causal force and meaning. Rather it is a third alternative, a movement of hyper-meaning so far beyond all ordinary meaning that it takes on many of the characteristics ordinarily associated with causal force. This kind of signifying cannot be accounted for in terms of causal force and (ordinary) meaning; but neither can causal force and (ordinary) meaning be accounted for in terms of this kind of signifying.

12

Foucault as genealogist

(i)

Derrida's Post-Structuralism is the earliest and the pivotal version of Post-Structuralism, but it is not the only version. Another version of almost equal importance is the version associated with Foucault in his 'genealogical' period of the 1970s. In many respects, Foucault's 'genealogy' follows on from where his 'archaeology' left off, extending into new areas of discourse the campaign against science and humanism. Thus, 'genealogies . . . are precisely anti-sciences'; and 'genealogy [is] a form of history which accounts for the constitution of knowledges [*savoirs*], discourses, domains of objects, etc., without having to refer to a subject'.[1] But in other respects, there is a decisive philosophical difference between 'archaeology' and 'genealogy'. And although Foucault does not appear to be directly influenced by Derrida – and even displays considerable animosity towards Derrida – yet this difference is in the end analogous to the difference between Saussure's theory of 'langue' and Derrida's theory of Writing.[2]

The most obvious aspect of the difference between 'archaeology' and 'genealogy' is that the latter puts the emphasis upon power rather than upon knowledge, upon practices rather than upon language. Thus Foucault now proposes that 'one's point of reference should not be to the great model of language [langue] and signs, but to that of war and battle'.[3] And apropos of the 'genealogical' concept of 'apparatus', he claims that 'what I call an apparatus is a much more general case of the *episteme*; or rather . . . the *episteme* is a specifically *discursive* apparatus, whereas the apparatus in its general form is both discursive and non-discursive'.[4] Of course, the connection between language and practices has always been crucial to Foucault's concept of discourse, and the connection between knowledge and power has always been crucial to his arguments against 'truth'. But with the new emphasis, there is a shift away from the notion of epistemic frameworks existing *in idea*, and a shift towards materialism. Power is to be directly related to bodies: 'What I am after is to try to show how the relations of power are able to pass materially into the very density of bodies without even having to be relayed by the representation of subjects.'[5] This shift towards materialism is analogous to the shift towards materialism in Derrida's Post-Structuralism.

The direct relation between power and bodies can be seen as operating in either of two ways. One way is the way of power *over* bodies: 'Power relations have an immediate hold upon [the body], they invest it, mask it, train it, torture it, force it to carry out tasks, to perform ceremonies, to emit signs.'[6] According to Foucault, this kind of hold has increased enormously in modern times, with 'a veritable technological take-off in the productivity of power'.[7] Whereas pre-capitalist economies needed only an external power to punish and tax bodies, the capitalist economy needs to force bodies to a new kind of labour, to extract productive service from them. And this involves an actual 'incorporation' of power into the bodies of individuals, controlling their acts and attitudes and behaviour from within.[8] Characteristically, such 'incorporation' operates through language and signs; but the reality behind it is war-like and battle-like.

The other way of power is the way of the body's own power, the body's own force of Will and Desire. Such a power *of* the body opposes the power *over* bodies, and thereby represents, for Foucault, the source of all revolution. Here Foucault leaves behind the dilemma of his 'archaeological' period, the dilemma of epistemic frameworks which are on the one hand totally inescapable and on the other hand politically objectionable. In his 'genealogical' period, Foucault discovers a force which is not a thinking and is therefore not determined by epistemic frameworks. For Foucault as for Derrida, society's dominating *a priori* 'langue' is no longer the primary reality. There is a deeper reality to which we can be true.

Foucault's new terminology of Will and Desire is explicitly Nietzschean, and he consistently draws upon Nietzschean arguments when demonstrating the rationalizations of power and the reality of war and battle. But we must tread carefully here. For Nietzsche can be and has been interpreted in very different ways, and Foucault's is by no means the most accepted or most obvious interpretation. The Existentialists, for instance, assimilated Nietzschean irrationalism to their own 'I'-philosophy: Will and Desire became free will and subjective desire, experienced through the subjective 'lived body'. For Anglo-Saxons, on the other hand, Nietzschean irrationalism has usually seemed to tie in with scientific notions of evolution and the organism: Will and Desire become biological instincts, pre-programmed towards the survival of the species. Neither of these interpretations is relevant to Foucault; and the biological interpretation, in particular, can only reduce 'genealogy' to a state of hopeless self-contradiction.

In fact, 'genealogy' is not only at odds with the Anglo-Saxon interpretation of Nietzsche, but with the whole Anglo-Saxon way of thinking about the body which lies behind that interpretation. This is especially the case when Foucault analyses sexuality and overturns the notion of sexual instincts and the myth of their repression. According to the myth, our natural sexual instincts have been forcibly restrained and hidden during the past three centuries of bourgeois class-domination: 'modern puritanism imposed its triple edict of taboo, nonexistence, and silence'.[9] So it seems to us now that the truth of sex,

> lodged in our most secret nature, 'demands' only to surface; that if it fails to do so, this is because a constraint holds it in place, the violence of a power weights it down, and it can finally be articulated only at the price of a kind of liberation.[10]

But according to Foucault, our sexual instincts are not so natural after all. True to the essential Superstructuralist vision, he gives the cultural superstructure priority over the supposed biological base:

> We believe in the full constancy of instinctual life and imagine
> that it continues to exert its force indiscriminately in the
> present as it did in the past. But a knowledge of history easily
> disintegrates this unity, depicts its wavering course . . . We
> believe, in any event, that the body obeys the exclusive laws of
> physiology and that it escapes the influence of history, but
> this too is false. The body is molded by a great many distinct
> regimes.[11]

There is nothing fundamental or inevitable about our sexual
instincts.

By way of illustration, Foucault considers the sexuality of the
child, as revealed by Freudian psychoanalysis. This sexuality,
he argues, is there to be revealed only because it was first put
there, historically, during the eighteenth century. During this
period, according to Foucault, the sexuality of the child was
suddenly 'discovered', as evidenced by a whole new literature
on the topic, with precepts, observations, medical advice, clinical cases, outlines for reform and plans for ideal institutions.
Great efforts were devoted especially to the eradication of
masturbation amongst schoolboys. And the end-result of such
efforts was, inevitably, not eradication but intensification:
'sexuality through thus becoming an object of analysis and
concern, surveillance and control, engender[ed] at the same
time an intensification of each individual's desire for, in, and
over his body'.[12] In effect, the sexuality of the child was created
by an eighteenth-century discourse.

As for the sexuality of the child, so for sexuality in general.
According to Foucault, western society has always been
obsessed with telling the truth about sex, ever since the time of
the old Catholic confessional. And specifically in the last three
centuries, 'since the classical age, there has been a constant
optimization and an increasing valorization of the discourse on
sex'.[13] This discourse on sex, even when speaking *against* sex,
creates its own object just like the discourses discussed by
Foucault in his 'archaeological' period. And the object thus
created is sexuality or the idea of sex, a cultural object that
imposes itself on bodies. As Foucault asks of our modern
so-called 'sex': 'is it not rather a complex idea that was formed
inside the deployment of sexuality?'[14]

Our modern so-called 'sex' thus possesses many remarkable qualities that are by no means natural. Sex is

> that agency which appears to dominate us and that secret which seems to underlie all that we are, that point which enthralls us through the power it manifests and the meaning it conceals, and which we ask to reveal what we are and to free us from what defines us.[15]

It has become a source and centre of all meaningfulness, the most important truth in our lives. Instead of sex as desire, we now have a desire for sex – as something which is in itself desirable.

Under Foucault's analysis, then, power does not appear in the form of a negative repressive power; but it appears none the less. It appears in the form of a positive expansionist power, 'a power bent on generating forces, making them grow and ordering them, rather than one dedicated to impeding them, making them submit, or destroying them'.[16] Such a power takes charge, not by prohibition, but by regulatory intervention and 'management procedures'. And it encourages the spread of sexuality because it can penetrate deeper into the body with sexuality as its support. Thus in the case of the eighteenth-century campaign against masturbation:

> The child's 'vice' was not so much an enemy as a support; it may have been designated as the evil to be eliminated, but the extraordinary effort that went into the task that was bound to fail leads one to suspect that what was demanded of it was to persevere . . . rather than to disappear for good. Always relying on this support, power advanced, multiplied its relays and its effects. . . . In appearance, we are dealing with a barrier system; but in fact, all around the child, indefinite *lines of penetration* were disposed.[17]

In appearance, the eradication of masturbation is the goal, and knowledge and surveillance are merely the means to that goal; but in fact, it is knowledge and surveillance in themselves that are the goal.

As for the nineteenth and twentieth centuries, Foucault sees the management and regulation of sex depending upon the increasing proximity between 'scientia sexualis' and the biological sciences. For 'by virtue of this . . . proximity, some of the contents of biology and physiology were able to serve as a principle of normality for human sexuality'.[18] Sexual behaviour is no longer constrained under the notion of sin; instead it is constrained under the notion of the àbnormal, the pathological. And, of course, this rule of the 'truth' of nature is much harder to shrug off than the rule of an explicitly man-made morality. With our characteristic western obsession about being natural, we characteristically internalize the standards of biology and carry out our own self-surveillance and self-regulation. Even Freud, who in some ways opposed the simple division between the normal and the pathological, still gave us a standard to internalize and obey.

As against our characteristic western obsession about being natural, Foucault sets the oriental way of thinking about sex in term of an *ars erotica*. This latter way of thinking is not directed towards 'a healthy sexuality' or 'a complete and flourishing sexuality' or 'the lyricism of orgasm and the good feelings of bio-energy'; it is directed towards 'pleasure . . . considered . . . first and foremost in relation to itself' and 'pleasure, evaluated in terms of its intensity'.[19] Instead of sex as a servant of nature or a centre of truth, this is sexuality as an erotic art, a kind of playing, creative and deliberately artificial.

Here we approach the crux of Foucault's conception of the body – the primary power *of* the body that resists all imposed power *over* the body. In Foucault's words, 'the rallying point for the counter-attack against the deployment of sexuality ought not to be sex-desire but bodies and pleasures'.[20] The usual biological conception of the body explains sex-desire as following from the reproductive instincts, and pleasure as following from the satisfaction of desire. Pleasure here is merely an incidental by-product, a reward for carrying out the good work of evolutionary survival. Or in Freudian terms, pleasure is merely gratification, the relief of getting back down to a normal state of stasis and balance after a period of tension and imbalance. Foucault's conception completely inverts all such models. For Foucault, the primary power *of* the body must be seen as a seeking after pleasure. It is the seeking after pleasure which gives rise to desire, and it is desire which uses the physical body. And the intensities of pleasure sought after in this way are quite beyond mere animal gratifications, and quite unrelated to the evolutionary survival of the species. The primary power derives as it were from the top rather than from the bottom, putting the body into a state of perpetual imbalance and perpetual restlessness and perpetual onward motion. Instead of speaking of the body and its pleasures, we should perhaps speak more precisely of pleasure and its bodies.

What's emerging here, of course, is an analogy between Foucault's conception of the body and Derrida's conception of the signifier. For, as we have seen, Derrida's signifier is also in a state of perpetual imbalance and perpetual restlessness and perpetual onward motion. And this state follows from the logic of supplementarity, where what's added on endlessly supplants and leaves behind what was there in the first place – just as, in Foucault's conception, ever-new intensities of pleasure endlessly supplant and leave behind original animal gratifications. In spite of the apparent distance between bodies and signifiers, Foucault's conception actually has a very similar philosophical status to Derrida's conception. On the one hand, the body obviously does not exist like an *idea*; but on the other hand – and no doubt less obviously – it also does not exist like a *thing*. Rather, it is always being pulled out of itself, always toppling forward into newly opening spaces, always being drawn across boundaries. What comes first for Foucault is not the solidity of the body but the power of the body as a force, just as what comes first for Derrida is not the signifier as an entity but the process of signifying. Foucault, like Derrida, is a materialist only in a very special sense.

(ii)

Along with the dimension of pleasure, there is another, very different, dimension to Foucault's conception of the body: the dimension of politics. Power *of* the body and *over* the body is also power in a political sense. And since power *of* the body and *over* the body appears in even the most local and small-scale human relations, so too does politics. Politics is no longer restricted to the level of general class relations, but percolates down into domestic relations, schooling relations, parent–child relations, and of course sexual relations. (On this dimension too, sex is anything but biological.) As Foucault says, 'in thinking of the mechanisms of power, I am thinking rather of its capillary form of existence, the point where power reaches into the very grain of individuals'.[21] In his 'genealogical' period, Foucault sees politics everywhere.

However, this does not mean that Foucault is putting forward a political theory in the old sense. He is not putting forward a totalizing description of how society is, nor a utopian vision of how, in the general interest, it should be. Such theories depend upon precisely that kind of impartial objective knowing which Foucault has always condemned as illusory. Politics, in Foucault's conception, depends not upon impartiality but upon self-interest: it becomes a matter of tactics and strategy. And politics, in Foucault's conception, depends not upon knowing but upon desire: it becomes materialized in bodies. Bodies are also involved in the conception of politics as practical action – in demonstrations, for instance, and physical confrontation. Foucault, who admits to having been politicized by the 1968 student revolution in France, develops his conception of politics very much in relation to the new kind of politics which grew out of that upheaval.

At the same time, however, this self-interest is still not to be interpreted in terms of the subject as an individual; and this desire of the body is still not to be interpreted in terms of any mere gratification of biological needs. Such interpretations would render interest and desire essentially a-social and ultimately a-political. Indeed, such interpretations would typically suggest notions of minimal government and the private vote, on the old Anglo-Saxon model. But Foucault's politics is over and above the individual even as it is below and beneath society-as-a-whole. Whence, for example, the strange philosophical status of 'the great anonymous, almost unspoken strategies': 'the logic is perfectly clear, the aims decipherable, and yet it is often the case that no one is there to have invented them, and few who can be said to have formulated them'.[22] Such strategies, it seems, must be granted an objectified existence of their own, virtually independent of the individual calculations of those taking part in them.

What's at issue here can be illustrated by a concrete example from Foucault:

Imagine that in some factory or other there is a conflict between a worker and one of the bosses, and that this worker suggests to his comrades that some retribution is called for. This would not be a real act of popular justice unless the target and the potential outcome were integrated into the overall political struggle of the workers in that factory.[23]

Knocking down a boss is not by itself a political action, not if it is performed merely in personal terms, merely between individuals, merely out of an instinctive sense of grievance. As Foucault says, 'an act of popular justice cannot achieve its full significance unless it is clarified politically'.[24] The key word here is 'significance'. When an action is integrated into an overall political struggle, it assumes a kind of general *meaning*. In acts of retribution – as in demonstrations and confrontations – the body is political only when it is used as a symbol.

Of course, Foucault will not allow us to think of this general meaning as something in the minds of those taking part. But perhaps we can conceive it in terms of formal differences. A personal hostility between workers and bosses is like a particular causal difference: it can motivate the throwing of a punch, but it has no meaning. A meaning arises only when workers and bosses stand in a relation of absolute, formal difference, when what the workers *are* is what the bosses *are not*, and vice versa. Does not this kind of difference lie at the heart of all politics? And might not a purely physical action thus manage to point to something beyond itself?

In any event, the presence of such meaning once again reveals the distance between 'genealogy' and all philosophies of the 'natural' body, and once again establishes the connection between 'genealogy' and Superstructuralism. In particular, we can now see more clearly than ever just how 'genealogy' fits into the Post-Structuralist phase of Superstructuralism. We have already seen that there is a power *of* the body which is not a thinking and is therefore not determined by the dominant epistēmē. Now we can see that there is also a symbolism of the body which can be used in political action and can be turned against the dominant epistēmē. So, as in Derrida's theory of Writing, two levels of the sign emerge: an institutionalized level of socially controlled discourse, and an anti-institutional level of the body's own revolutionary symbolism.

The concept of the body's own revolutionary symbolism

underlies Foucault's account of the history of the penal system. According to Foucault, the modern penal system was erected against a 'danger' that appeared towards the end of the eighteenth century, the 'danger' of actions previously regarded as criminal starting to take on political meaning. Before and around and after the time of the French Revolution, 'a whole series of illegalities was inscribed in struggles in which those struggling knew that they were confronting both the law and the class that had imposed it'.[25] Refusing to pay rents, looting shops, attacking the king's agents – such hitherto individual retributions and confrontations were becoming integrated into a general protest against the existing state of society. But the invention of the modern penal system saved the day for social order and its new guardians, the bourgeoisie. With the modern penal system, the old methods of violent punishment were supplanted by more gentle but also more thorough methods of control: methods of routine, measurement, surveillance and observation. As Foucault puts it, 'The perpetual penality that traverses all points and supervises every instant in the disciplinary institutions compares, differentiates, hierarchizes, homogenizes, excludes. In short, it *normalizes*.'[26] Or to put it another way, the small ceaseless grind of prison existence crushes the meaning out of the bodies of prisoners.

Foucault thus inverts the accepted wisdom of penology, which claims a relative humanity for the new methods of control and which proposes as the goal of imprisonment not punishment for its own sake but the *reform* of the criminal. As Foucault points out, such reform has never been achieved; the modern penal system seems only to encourage recidivism. How, then, has so consistently unsuccessful a system managed to survive? Foucault suggests that it has survived because it has actually proved very successful in terms of another, quite unstated goal – the positive production of delinquency:

> For the observation that prison fails to eliminate crime, one should perhaps substitute the hypothesis that prison has succeeded extremely well in producing delinquency, a specific type, a politically or economically less dangerous – and, on occasion, usable – form of illegality . . . in producing the delinquent as a pathologized subject.[27]

Delinquency is less dangerous because it is merely personal and local and limited in its power to attract popular support. For a strategy of social order this advantage far outweighs the very minor disadvantage of habitualizing criminals to a lifelong cycle of crime and imprisonment. Just as the eighteenth-century campaign against childhood sexuality succeeded even as it failed to eradicate masturbation, so the modern penal system succeeds even as it fails to eradicate crime. In both cases, there is 'a mastery of [the body's] forces that is more than the ability to conquer them'.[28]

If the strategy of social order works in terms of its practical means rather than in terms of its programmatic goal, so too with the countervailing strategy of social disorder. Foucault seeks to recover a revolutionary political meaning for prisoners and other 'normalized' minorities, but he does not seek to proclaim a goal towards which revolutionary political action should aim. The revolutionary political meaning of prisoners and other minorities is simply the meaning of a difference between the minority and the law, between the minority and the class which has imposed the law; it is the negative meaning of what the minority is *against* rather than a positive meaning of what the minority is *for*. With Foucault, politicization has become an end in itself: 'the problem is not so much that of defining a political 'position' (which is to choose from a pre-existing set of possibilities) but to imagine and bring into being new schemes of politicisation'.[29] There is no blue-print for a post-revolutionary state of society in Foucault's writings.

In so far as one may deduce a post-revolutionary state of society from Foucault's writings at all, it seems clear that there can be no once-and-for-all removal of power-relations. Power is too deeply ingrained, it is 'always already there'; and Foucault's Nietzschean way of thinking gives no reason to suppose that the power *of* some bodies would ever cease to entail a power *over* other bodies. If a post-revolutionary state of society is to represent any improvement over the existing state, it must be by virtue of a loosening and unstructuring of power-relations: power-relations would still exist, but in ever-changing ever-flowing forms. There would be no permanent appropriations of power. Indeed, power-relations might even be envisaged in terms of creative play, whereby controls would be set up only in order to be transgressed.

This way of thinking, in so far as one may deduce it from Foucault's writings, seems more appropriate to a specifically French tradition of revolution – as exemplified by the French Revolution and the 1870 Paris Commune – than to the tradition of Communist revolution – as exemplified by the 1917 Russian Revolution. (Here it is perhaps worth noting that Foucault's attitude to prison and prisoners looks very much like a throw-back to Fourierism.) In fact, Foucault is avowedly anti-Marxist: not only when he rejects the reduction of all power-relations to class-relations, but also when he rejects the ideal of an ultimate social harmony and the belief in an inevitable historical progression towards that ideal. Such rejections stem from a fundamentally different conception of human existence. In one particularly revealing lecture, for instance, Foucault even claims that

> it is false to say, 'with that famous post-Hegelian' [Marx], that the concrete existence of man is labour. For the life and time of man are not by nature labour, but pleasure, restless-ness, merry-making, rest, needs, accidents, desires, violent acts, robberies, etc.[30]

And he goes on to speak of man's 'quite explosive, momentary and discontinuous energy'.[31] Clearly, this unpredictable and irresponsible dynamism must find expression in any 'true' state of society.

Of course, what divides Foucault from Marx relates Foucault, once again, to Derrida. For there is a similar dyna-mism in Derrida's theory of Writing: as we have seen, linguistic meaning as disseminated is perpetually in motion, it reaches no terminus, it is forever toppling across boundaries. Derrida opens language up to an anarchic proliferation of forms over and above anyone's deliberate intentions, just as Foucault opens politics up to an anarchic proliferation of forms over and above anyone's deliberate aims or goals. And if we view Derrida's theory of Writing as an unrestricted version of Hegel's self-generating logic, might we not similarly view Foucault's approach to politics as an unrestricted version of Hegel's self-generating history of political systems?

13

More Post-Structuralists

(i)

As Foucault moves from a version of Structuralism to a version of Post-Structuralism, so too do Kristeva and Barthes. But Kristeva and Barthes are concerned with language rather than with politics. Thus their version of Structuralism is a semiotics founded originally upon Saussure, and their version of Post-Structuralism is a philosophy of meaning derived mainly from Derrida. Kristeva, for instance, began with aspirations to a universal mathematical understanding of signs, while Barthes envisaged an all-encompassing science of culture and society. But both came up against the problem already described in Section (i) of Chapter 10, the problem of a 'science of an object ("language", "speech" or "discourse") so obedient to the necessity for social communication as to be inseparable from sociality'.[1] Seeking an escape from such all-encompassing social control, Kristeva and Barthes abandon the old 'euphoric dream of scientificity', and turn their attention to possible forms of transgressive anti-social creativity.[2]

At first sight, of course, the escape from social control can look like a mere return to individualism, especially when Kristeva insists upon the reintroduction of 'the speaking subject' and Barthes insists upon 'the freedom of the Reader'. However, this freedom is not the free will of a transcendental consciousness, and this subject is not the coherent subject of a self or an 'I'. On the contrary, 'the speaking subject' is 'a divided subject, even a pluralized subject, that occupies, not a place of enunciation, but permutable, multiple, and mobile places'.[3] Indeed, Kristeva also claims that 'the subject never *is*, the *subject* is only the *process* of *signification*'.[4] Once again, the forms of creativity are to be ultimately located in language itself, language as it only *passes through* individuals.

Kristeva and Barthes therefore separate out two distinct levels of language: a level of 'signifiance' or creative transgressive meaning, and a level of 'signification' or socially instituted socially controlled meaning. On the former level, 'the text is . . . a *productivity*', according to Kristeva; and, according to Barthes, 'the text only exists in the movement of a discourse . . . *the Text is experienced only in an activity of production*'.[5] Whereas the 'signification' of a word is held fixed and self-identical within a system, the 'signifiance' of a word opens out centrifugally. As Kristeva puts it, 'it is necessary . . . to decompose [the sign] and to open up within its interior a new outside, a new space of malleable and combinatory sites, the space of *signifiance*'.[6] Barthes supplies the perfect metaphor when he speaks of 'running' the structure of a system like the thread of a stocking.[7]

'Signifiance' opens out in two ways. One way is the way of what Kristeva calls 'intertextuality'. 'Intertextuality' depends upon the notion that 'in the space of a given text, several utterances taken from other texts intersect and neutralize one another'.[8] Reading for 'signifiance', we undo this neutralization and 'run' the threads of meaning back across all the other texts from which our given text was formed. Hence a perpetual multiplication of meaning, as for the 'polyvalent and multi-determined' poetic word, which 'adheres to a logic exceeding that of codified discourse'.[9] Only on the socially controlled level can language be held down to single meanings.

The other way of 'signifiance' is the way of the body. Thus Barthes insists upon a corporeal level of reading, where meaning is 'run' and multiplied through the reader's body. 'The pleasure of the text is that moment when my body pursues its own ideas.'[10] Kristeva, for her part, discovers the 'geno-text', where meaning operates in an archaic, inchoate mode, before and beyond communication or syntax or language in the ordinary sense: 'these "operations" are *pre-meaning* and *pre-sign* (or *trans-meaning* and *trans-sign*)'.[11] And Kristeva relates these operations to instinctual drives and even to the biological organism: 'they bring us back to a process of division in the living organism'.[12] Such operations perpetually cross and transgress the fixed categories of 'signification'.

But when Kristeva and Barthes talk of body and drives and organism, the terms are to be taken in a very special sense. Thus we may notice that Barthes's conception of the body does not preclude 'ideas', and that although Kristeva refers to the process of division in the living organism, she does not refer to the equally important process of self-stabilization. (Purely by itself, the process of division is the process of a cancer.) In fact, body and organism are here being used essentially as terms for expressing the materiality of the Freudian Unconscious; and the materiality of the Freudian Unconscious is, once again, the very special materiality of signifiers signifying. Kristeva, for instance, speaks of 'bio-physiological processes (themselves already inescapably part of signifying processes; what Freud labelled "drives")'.[13] We must no longer think of drives merely as the urge to gratify animal needs, but as the desire of signifying and the signifying of desire. Thus the two ways of 'signifiance' rejoin one another; the way of the body is ultimately the same as the way of 'intertextuality'.

This is all very obviously analogous to Derrida's philosophy of language. There are the same two levels of meaning, the socially controlled level versus the anti-socially creative level. And the anti-socially creative level has all the features that Derrida attributes to Writing: meaning is in motion instead of static, it is multiple instead of single, and it is material instead of mental. Even the two ways of 'signifiance' correspond to the two aspects of Writing which emerge under Derrida's special theory and general theory respectively. Kristeva and Barthes clarify certain points in Derrida's philosophy of language, but they do not change its overall outline. They are original thinkers mainly when they extend this philosophy into the field of literary criticism. But into this field we shall not follow them.

(ii)

If Kristeva and Barthes relate especially to Derrida's version of Post-Structuralism, Deleuze and Guattari relate especially to Foucault's version. In the latter casè, though, Deleuze and Guattari have probably influenced Foucault at least as much as he has influenced them. In particular, the characteristic Nietzscheanism of this version seems to have been first introduced by Deleuze in his earlier solo works, *Nietzsche et la philosophie* (P.U.F., 1962) and *Différence et répétition* (P.U.F., 1968). As for Deleuze and Guattari as a duo, they share many philosophical and political attitudes with Foucault, but apply themselves to their own distinctive area of analysis – namely, psychoanalysis.

In the area of psychoanalysis, Deleuze and Guattari carry the Lacanian revolution even further. Unlike Lacan, they no longer claim to be returning to Freud. On the contrary, they define their position in opposition to Freud, and value Lacan only in so far as he re-thinks Freud. Where he does not re-think Freud they condemn him; and most of all they condemn him for accepting the assumptions of Oedipalism.

Oedipalism, in this context, is that mode of symbolic interpretation which regresses all phenomena of the Unconscious back to the primal family triangle of 'mommy-daddy-me'. Thus the many different people in dreams are typically interpreted as covert representations of just two people in real life – the mother and the father – and the many different events in dreams are typically interpreted as covert manifestations of just one underlying desire – incestuous sexual desire. Deleuze and Guattari, however, regard incestuous sexual desire as 'a *slandered shallow stream*', and claim that 'the first error of psychoanalysis is in acting as if things began with the child'.[14] From their point of view, Oedipalism appears as a false attempt to reduce the Unconscious to some single constant centre, some essential original base. From their point of view, Lacan superstructuralizes the Unconscious when he disconnects it from the biological or animal instincts; but he fails to carry his superstructuralizing through to its logical conclusions. Like Saussure who grounds language upon oral language, like Lévi-Strauss who grounds culture upon primitive culture, Lacan still wants to ground the Unconscious upon primal experience within the 'natural' family. In the end, he falls back upon the old assumption that what's most important is what comes first.

Deleuze and Guattari superstructuralize the Unconscious to a further degree altogether. As they see it, the Unconscious is not individually generated out of private family experience, but socially generated out of collective public experience. 'Fantasy is never individual: it is *group fantasy*.'[15] The meanings of the Unconscious are on a par with every other kind of meaning that spreads across society as a whole. And such meanings no more refer to individuals than they belong to individuals: 'the Unconscious is totally unaware of persons as such'.[16] What the Unconscious knows are social and political roles: the Chinaman, the Arab, the black, the cop, the occupier, the collaborator, the radical, the resister, the boss, the boss's wife. Public and historical events too: Stalinism, the Vietnam War, the rise of fascism.[17] Such figures and events – familiar enough in dreams – do not need to be brought down to elemental terms before they can be allowed to take up residence in the Unconscious. On the contrary, 'all delirium possesses a world-historical, political, and racial content'.[18] If anything, it is the figure of the mother and the figure of the father that need to be spread out and interpreted in social and political terms.

With this kind of an Unconscious as the underlying truth of human nature, we can no longer take our bearings from those traditional reference-points, the child and the primitive. It is not the child or the primitive who live especially close to this kind of an Unconscious – but the schizophrenic. By a typical Post-Structuralist paradox, the underlying truth of human nature appears most fully in a mental condition peculiarly characteristic of the most 'unnatural' and highly developed state of twentieth-century western capitalist society. In Deleuze and Guattari's 'schizoanalysis', the schizophrenic actually becomes the new 'Homo natura', from whom we must take our bearings. Needless to say, this is a complete inversion of orthodox psychoanalysis, where schizophrenia is seen as something to be cured. But it is not an altogether surprising consequence of the general development of Superstructuralist thinking. There has always been a potential analogy to be drawn between the Superstructuralists' way of *theorizing* the world and the schizophrenic's way of *living* it.

In the first place, the schizophrenic lives the world *as signs*. For him, there are neither people nor things but meanings, endlessly and everywhere. He may seem to be hearing people always talking about him, he may seem to be receiving special messages from God, he may seem to be starring in a great world-wide film about himself – all these and many other variations can be derived from a basic tendency to over-reading or hyper-interpretation. And recent studies have increasingly concentrated upon this tendency as the very essence of schizo-phrenia. Even Anglo-Saxon studies, as by Lidz and Wynne and especially Bateson, now view schizophrenia as primarily a kind of communication disorder. But in relation to the Superstruc-turalists' way of theorizing the world, of course, this disorder is hardly a disorder at all. In relation to the Superstructuralists' way of theorizing the world, this disorder is potentially closer to the true state of affairs than is our 'normal' filtered admission of meanings.

Another basic schizoid tendency is the tendency to self-fragmentation. Sometimes this may take the form of a 'split personality', in the old and popular conception; sometimes it may take the form of an 'identification' with, say, Joan of Arc or the Great Mongol. (According to Deleuze and Guattari, this latter effect is produced by the passage of a Joan-of-Arc or Great-Mongol meaning, rather than by any kind of *personal* identification.)[19] These and many other variations can be de-rived from the schizophrenic's characteristic failure to hold his behaviour and states of mind together under a conscious en-compassing 'I'. Indeed, as Deleuze and Guattari point out, he often refuses to speak the word 'I', and prefers to refer to himself in the third person.[20] In relation to the Superstructuralist's way of theorizing the world, of course, this disorder is once again potentially closer to the true state of affairs than is our 'normal' sense of self.

What makes the schizophrenic especially significant for Post-Structuralists is that he is anti-social *as well as* social. He is social because of his openness to public collective meanings, but he is anti-social because of his rejection of all conventional codes and structures. In fact, he has never been taken over by that socially instituted, socially controlled language which, according to Lacan, overtakes the growing child from the age of eighteen months on. He refuses to deal with social meanings as society would have them dealt with: he turns them *against* society. And this of course fits in very neatly with the general Post-Structuralist notion of a deeper subversive level of meaning undermining the dominant accepted level.

The schizophrenic refuses to deal with social meanings as society would have them dealt with because he refuses to observe *boundaries* between them. From a 'normal' point of view, this tendency appears as defective category formation and muddled thinking by association. But for Deleuze and Guattari it represents an alternative logic, a non-exclusive logic of 'either . . . or . . . or' in place of the old exclusive logic of 'either/or':

> Whereas the 'either/or' claims to mark decisive choices between immutable terms (the alternative: either this or that), the schizophrenic 'either . . . or . . . or' refers to the system of possible permutations between differences that always amount to the same as they shift and slide about.[21]

It is not that the schizophrenic is simply unaware of differences between, say, the self and the other, the child and the parents. (Anyone simply unaware of such differences would be simply incapable of language and simply sub-human.) But the schizophrenic is aware of the differences only to cross over them; he recognizes the boundaries only to transgress them. When the schizophrenic 'becomes' his own parent, he is *living* the ultimate linguistic dependence of one meaning (self, child) upon its opposite (other, parent). 'He is child *or* parent, not both, but the one at the end of the other, like the two ends of a stick in a nondecomposable space.'[22] He can neither stay with just one meaning nor unify both meanings together, but must perpetually glide across the difference between them – and then across all the other differences that both depend upon in relation to all other meanings in language. Thus meaning on the schizophrenic's level is in a never-ending state of flux and mutation, restlessly producing itself, restlessly picking up its roots and moving on. In the words of Deleuze and Guattari, 'The signifying chain has become a chain of decoding and deterritorialization, which must be apprehended – and can only be apprehended – as the reverse of the codes and the territorialities.'[23] What appears from a 'normal' point of view as an unfortunate incapacity for concentration and steady centred thinking appears to Deleuze and Guattari as a fortunate capacity for setting meaning in motion and making it multiply. Meaning on the schizophrenic's level is in precisely that state to which all Post-Structuralists aspire.

Not only is meaning on the schizophrenic's level in motion and multiplying, it is also in a way material. For the schizophrenic, as Freud himself recognized, tends to take words for things. Words received are received like physical stimuli: 'all words become physical and affect the body immediately'; and words produced are produced like physical acts: '[the language-sign] is still a sign, but one that merges with an action or passion of the body'.[24] This tendency reveals to Deleuze and Guattari a truth upon which they ground their whole philosophy: the truth that meanings in the Unconscious are simply meanings as *workings of the body*. Freud thus made a grave mistake when he turned his back upon the schizophrenic and allowed himself to think of meanings in the Unconscious as images or ghosts or signifieds performing (albeit behind the curtain) on an inner mental stage. 'The unconscious ceases to be what it is – a factory, a workshop – to become a theatre, a scene and its staging.'[25] According to Deleuze and Guattari, the truth of the Unconscious is the truth of a machine-like solidity: 'the unconscious . . . engineers, it is machinic'.[26]

But although this conception of meaning is material and machine-like, it is, like Derrida's, material and machine-like only in a very special sense. For Deleuze and Guattari, matter and machines are never *inert* as for the natural scientist or technologist. They do not think in terms of predetermining arrangements of matter through which a causal clockwork runs. Such 'mechanistic' notions are entirely foreign to their own 'machinic' notion.[27] Instead they emphasize the *force* of a machine over and above its *matter*, to the point where the force of a machine becomes quite unpredictable, excessive and insatiable. It is in such a condition that the force of a machine can be equated with the force of desire – whence Deleuze and Guattari's paradoxical talk of 'desiring-machines'. In fact, such 'desiring-machines' are not only not determined by their matter, but actually consume their matter in the production of force. 'Desiring-machines . . . continually break down as they run', say Deleuze and Guattari, 'and ... the parts of the machine are the fuel that makes it run.'[28] Such assertions have nothing to do with our ordinary orderly hard-working machines. These machines are wild machines, exploding machines.

Of course, not all schizophrenics live with the force of a wild machine. What Deleuze and Guattari are here promoting is the schizophrenic's potential rather than his typical behaviour under present-day conditions. In fact, many schizophrenics live in a very force-less state of silence and closure and catatonia. But according to Deleuze and Guattari, this is merely a secondary state, brought about by a society which medicalizes schizophrenia, blocks it off and turns it in upon itself. The schizophrenic still has the essential capacity of being able to let go and give himself up to the motion and multiplying and machine-like force of meaning. For he does not fear the 'madness' that 'normal' members of society fear, he is not neurotic in the way that 'normal' members of society are neurotic. And in the end, according to Deleuze and Guattari, *'the only incurable is the neurotic'.*[29]

In so far as our twentieth-century western capitalist society is a society which medicalizes and blocks off schizophrenia, Deleuze and Guattari condemn it. But in so far as our twentieth-century western capitalist society is also a society which breeds this schizophrenia in the first place, they cannot simply dismiss it. Clearly there is a double process here. In one movement, our society conduces towards schizophrenia because of its uniquely restless and rootless nature: 'everything in the system is insane; this is because the capitalist machine thrives on decoded and deterritorialized flows'.[30] Specifically, the capitalist machine thrives on 'the decoded flows of production in the form of money-capital and the decoded flows of labour in the form of the "free worker"'.[31] Deleuze and Guattari here take exactly the contrary tack to the earlier Structuralists and Semioticians, and emphasize the degree to which our society has shrugged off the falsely imposed structures characteristic of all previous societies. At the same time, however, they recognize an opposing movement whereby our society represses schizophrenia and reimposes control: *'what* [civilized modern societies] *deterritorialize with one hand, they reterritorialize with the other'.*[32] Such reterritorialization operates especially within the nuclear family, and especially through the structures of Oedipalization. With the aid of these even more falsely imposed structures, our society attempts to stave off the consequences of its own real nature.

The new way of looking at twentieth-century western capitalist society is accompanied by a new way of looking at political revolution. For instead of wanting to reverse the trend of capitalism, Deleuze and Guattari want to push it on still further, beyond Oedipalization and into schizophrenization. They want it to live out the consequences of its own real nature:

> For perhaps the flows are not yet deterritorialized enough, not decoded enough, from the viewpoint of a theory and a practice of a highly schizophrenic character. Not to withdraw from the process, but to go further, to 'accelerate the process', as Nietzsche put it: in this matter, the truth is that we haven't seen anything yet.[33]

Under this new way of looking (which appears also in another recent French theorist, Lyotard), political revolution follows a Post-Structuralist logic of supplementarity.

(iii)

Yet another version of Post-Structuralism appears in the writings of Baudrillard. Like Foucault and Deleuze and Guattari, Baudrillard takes a political approach to things, but his political approach is somewhat different. Indeed, when he attacks Foucault and Deleuze and Guattari, he emphasizes the difference until it looks quite unbridgeable.[34] But this is essentially faction-fighting, like the faction-fighting between Foucault and Derrida, and should not blind us to the general theoretical position that Baudrillard none the less shares in common with other Post-Structuralists.

In the writings of his earlier phase, Baudrillard's main reference point is Marx, just as Deleuze and Guattari's main reference point is Freud. And just as Deleuze and Guattari continue Lacan's superstructuralization of psychoanalysis until they end up in complete opposition to Freud, so Baudrillard continues Althusser's superstructuralization of political economy until he ends up in complete opposition to Marx. Baudrillard seeks to overthrow not merely an 'economistic' emphasis that can be ascribed to Marx's interpreters but the whole founding conception of 'use-value' which belongs undeniably to Marx himself.

In Marx's conception, 'use-value' is value measured in terms of man's relation to a concrete outside world, as distinct from 'exchange-value' which is value measured in terms of exchange-relations between man and man. Baudrillard rejects this conception because he does not accept that there is a concrete outside world in the ordinary sense at all. For Baudrillard, 'the "real" table does not exist'.[35] Like Plato or Hegel, he regards the concrete outside world as an illusion or secondary effect: 'The empirical "object", given in its contingency of form, color, material, function and discourse . . . is a myth. . . . It is nothing but the different types of relations and significations that converge, contradict themselves, and twist around it.'[36] Needless to say, this is a position of the very highest metaphysical idealism.

Baudrillard also has more specific objections to the two possible ways of measuring value in terms of man's relation to a concrete outside world: the measurement by natural needs (which man must satisfy from the concrete outside world) and the measurement by natural labour-power (which man must apply to the concrete outside world). As for natural needs, he argues that no needs are so natural that human beings will not readily give them up for non-functional purposes, even in the most primitive living conditions:

> In fact, the 'vital anthropological minimum' doesn't exist: in all societies, it is determined residually by the fundamental urgency of an excess: the divine or sacrificial share, sumptuous discharge, economic profit. . . . And the priority of this claim works everywhere at the expense of the functional side of the balance sheet – at the expense, where necessary, of minimal subsistence.[37]

Carrying the French anthropological tradition to its extreme, Baudrillard claims that needs have always been entirely secondary to the primary reality of social exchange: 'For the primitives, eating, drinking, and living are first of all acts that are exchanged: if they are not exchanged, they do not occur.'[38]

As for natural labour-power, Baudrillard considers work no more important than non-functional play and ritual, even in the most primitive living conditions. Whereas Marx thinks of man as alienated only when he has to hire out his labour-power, Baudrillard thinks of man as alienated when he starts to see himself in terms of labour-power in the first place.[39]

From Baudrillard's point of view, Marx is in fact caught up in the preconceptions of the very system he is trying to attack. Thus, when Marx defines the working class by its labour-power, he is agreeing to 'an essence which in fact [the working class] was assigned by the bourgeois class'.[40] He is still under the spell of the bourgeois work-ethic. And when he wields the principle of needs against the interests of capital, his weapon is a mirage that was invented and promoted by capital precisely to serve its own interests. He is still under the spell of the capitalist consumption-ethic. In these respects, Marx's attack on the Classical economists is not nearly radical enough.

From Baudrillard's point of view, Marx also fails to overturn the Classical economists' conception of what constitutes a proper relationship between use-value and exchange-value. For Marx attacks only the Classical economists' belief that such a relationship actually occurs in capitalist economies. In Marx's conception, the apparent fairness and balance in exchange-relations between man and man no longer corresponds to a real fairness and balance on the level of use-value; the system of equivalences on the level of exchange-value merely obscures and excuses the real exploitation of one class by another. But Marx still thinks that exchange-value *ought* to correspond to use-value. The relative autonomy of exchange-value in capitalist economies is something of which he disapproves.

Baudrillard has quite different grounds for disapproval. He does not object to an improper relationship between use-value and exchange-value; in his theory, exchange-value *is* autonomous. What he objects to is exchange-value *per se*, exchange-value as it operates in capitalist economies, exchange-value *as a system of equivalences*. He objects to the way in which everything under the system is coded and measured and regulated and pinned down to an economic value. For Baudrillard, this is a tyranny much more serious than the mere accumulation of material benefits by one class at the expense of another; this is a tyranny that strikes at the proper functioning of social exchange, the very essence of human existence. And it is by referring everything to natural needs, natural labour-power and natural use-value that this tyranny manages to make itself seem natural. Baudrillard therefore inverts the notion that exchange-value obscures and excuses a real exploitation on the level of use-value, and claims that, on the contrary, use-value serves as 'a referential rationale (*raison*), a content, an alibi' for a real tyranny on the level of exchange-value.[41]

This tyranny, according to Baudrillard, has become especially obvious with the development of the capitalist economies in the twentieth century. In Marx's day, the system of equivalences applies only to the exchange of material products. But the capitalist economies have since moved into a wholly new phase: 'a revolution has occurred in the capitalist world without our Marxists having wanted to comprehend it'.[42] Now the measuring, coding, regulating system applies to every aspect of human exchange-relations. Even sexuality and recreation have been progressively systematized.[43] The capitalist economies have moved 'from the form-commodity to the form-sign, from the abstraction of the exchange of material products under the law of general equivalence to the operationalization of all exchanges under the law of the code'.[44] We thus live under a regime of controlled signs, in a condition of increasing 'social abstraction'. And this is a much more parlous condition than Marx ever contemplated. What we are now faced with is 'a structure of control and of power much more subtle and more totalitarian than that of exploitation'.[45] What we are now faced with is 'the symbolic destruction of all social relations not so much by the ownership of the means of production but by *the control of the code*'.[46] From a twentieth-century perspective, the material exploitation that Marx assailed appears as merely a passing phase in the growth of something much larger and more threatening – the tyranny of the code itself.

Like other Post-Structuralists, Baudrillard thus finds intolerable that very condition of modern society which the Structuralist Semioticians merely, scientifically, describe; and, like other Post-Structuralists, he looks for an alternative. But, as always, this alternative is not to be found in some simple pre-signifying 'nature'; it is to be found in a further intensification of signifying

itself. Like other Post-Structuralists, Baudrillard thus distinguishes two different levels of signifying: on the one hand,
the rigid structured level of 'signification' and 'the sign', on the
other hand, the free-flowing level of the 'symbolic' and 'the
symbol'.

The two levels differ because, in the first place, 'the sign' is
pinned down to a single meaning whereas 'the symbol' is
charged with a multiplicity of meanings. For instance, the sun
as a *symbol* has the 'ambivalence of a natural force – life and
death, beneficent and murderous'.[47] Such is the sun of the
primitive cults, the sun of the Aztecs and the Egyptians, the sun
of the peasant labourer. The sun as a *sign*, on the other hand, has
been reduced to a single-minded positivity, 'the absolute source
of happiness and euphoria, and as such ... significantly
opposed to non-sun (rain, cold, bad weather)'.[48] Such is the sun
of the modern vacationer, the sun as presented in holiday and
travel advertising. Similarly in the case of the body. According
to Baudrillard, the body is a *symbol* when the *act* of unclothing
reveals 'the true path of desire, which *is always ambivalent*, love
and death simultaneously'.[49] The body is a *sign*, on the other
hand, when our 'functional modern nudity' reveals only 'a body
entirely positivized by sex – as a cultural value, as a model of
fulfillment, as an emblem, as a morality (or ludic immorality,
which is the same thing)'.[50] This nudity is a kind of clothing
even as it differentiates itself from clothing; it takes on value in
the same fixed equational system of fashion and status. In such
ways, according to Baudrillard, '*all ambivalence is reduced by
equivalence*'.[51]

As 'the symbol' is not a simple positive value, so 'symbolic
exchange' is not an exchange of equivalent values. According to
Baudrillard, 'symbolic exchange' works by the principle of the
gift – the principle described by Marcel Mauss in his studies of
primitive exchange. According to Baudrillard, the principle of
the gift is quite antithetical to the principle of use-value and the
principle of (economic) exchange-value. For the gift, on the
giver's side, represents pure loss and wastage: 'the exchange-
gift *lost* and *given* without economic calculation of return and
compensation'.[52] And the gift, on the receiver's side, is not a
value to be measured against other values: 'objects or categories
of goods cathected in the singular and personal act of symbolic

exchange (the gift, the present) are strictly incomparable. The personal relation (non-economic exchange) renders them absolutely unique.'[53] To give and receive gifts in what we still recognize as 'the proper spirit' is to strike a blow against all measuring, coding, regulating systems. (Of course, 'the proper spirit' is not always observed even in primitive societies, as witness Lévi-Strauss's account of the orgies of uncalculating gift-giving amongst tribes of Nambikwara Indians – and the subsequent declarations of war when one tribe retrospectively calculates that it has received less than its fair share!)[54]

What matters with the gift, then, is not the value of the *thing* but the *act* of giving and receiving. The gift, in its movement from person to person, asserts the priority of relationship: 'In symbolic exchange, of which the gift is our most proximate illustration, the object is not an object: it is inseparable from the concrete relation in which it is exchanged, the transferential pact that it seals between two persons.'[55] The movement of the gift is true to the essential autonomy of social exchange, exchange for the sake of exchange. Even the positions of giver and receiver are mere moments of the movement, endlessly changing and reciprocating. There can be no fixed sites of individual accumulation in this free-flowing state. 'Symbolic exchange' represents for Baudrillard a triumph of process over stasis – yet another version of the characteristic Post-Structuralist emphasis.

However, it is clear that societies of 'the symbol' and 'symbolic exchange' belong essentially to the past. When Baudrillard describes this free-flowing state in the writings of his earlier phase, he does not present it as a state to which modern society is ever likely to return. If our present-day regime of 'the sign' is to be overcome at all, it must be by a very different route. And, in the writings of his later phase, Baudrillard explores the possibility of just such a route.

The possibility that Baudrillard explores is the possibility of embracing the regime of 'the sign' so completely as to push it into a position of unsustainable excess. If we can no longer simply recover a state of social flow and giving, then we must take the deliberately perverse route of intensifying our present-day state of anti-social inertia and passive receptivity. And, since consumerism is the very essence of our anti-social inertia and passive receptivity, we must become more purely consumers than ever:

> a system is abolished only by pushing it into hyperlogic, by forcing it into an excessive practice which is equivalent to a brutal amortization. 'You want us to consume – O.K., let's consume always more, and anything whatsoever; for any useless and absurd purpose.'[56]

This attitude, according to Baudrillard, is already the attitude of 'the masses' – 'the masses' as created by modern mass-society. In Baudrillard's metaphors, 'the masses' are truly like a physical dead weight, absorbing everything and responding to nothing. According to Baudrillard, consumption for 'the masses' has become a mere game and politics has become a mere spectacle. Bombarded with signs from the mass media, they no longer treat such signs as standing for anything meaningful. Yet our political system still depends upon the *presumption* of meaning, and our consumer system still depends upon the *alibi* of use-value. So, by taking signs *literally*, as nothing more than signs, 'the masses', according to Baudrillard, are driving the regime of 'the sign' towards its own logical self-destruction.

However, the role of 'the masses' is here entirely negative. Unlike Marx's proletariat, Baudrillard's 'masses' carry no seed from which a more positive state of society might spring, after the self-destruction of our present state. In fact, more positive states of society do not really feature on Baudrillard's agenda at all. His thinking is essentially nihilistic; he seems to welcome the prospect of a final apocalypse, and his main concern is to have it arrive as soon as possible. Behind the perverse route that Baudrillard proposes for overcoming the regime of 'the sign', there lies an even deeper, grander perversity.

Although such perversity is not without Post-Structuralist antecedents, Baudrillard clearly goes beyond Post-Structuralism here. Indeed, Baudrillard's later writings could even be regarded as a whole new twist of the Superstructuralist screw, a Post-Post-Structuralism as it were. But if so, this whole new twist does not as yet appear to have generated any great ferment in the French intellectual world, at least not on a par with the ferment of Structuralism and Post-Structuralism. Baudrillard's later writings seem to be closing doors rather than opening them.

Conclusion

In the Introduction, I claimed that the Superstructuralist epistēmē does not have a simple centralized unity and cannot be focused upon any single central text or moment or programme. We can now more clearly specify the particular kind of unity that it does have. The unity of Superstructuralism is the unity of a developing story.

This developing story is no mere straightforward sequence of expansions and conquests. We are not looking at some given approach applied more and more widely to ever further fields of study. Of course, such expansions and conquests do occur within the Superstructuralist story, especially during the earlier Structuralist phase. Thus we can see how Structuralist Linguistics spreads its influence into the fields of anthropology and literary criticism, and ultimately into the all-encompassing field of general Semiotics. But (*pace* the Anglo-Saxon Semioticians) the story of Superstructuralism as a whole cannot be understood in such simple horizontal terms.

To understand the story of Superstructuralism as a whole we have to recognize that the Superstructuralist approach has itself changed and developed. We have to recognize a vertical process of auto-critique and internal reformulation: not merely expanding all-on-a-level, but deepening down from level to level. Time and again, Superstructuralism has advanced by seeing more clearly into its own underlying assumptions, by facing up to the radical implications of those assumptions, and by purging itself of ordinary ways of thinking ultimately incompatible with those assumptions. From Saussure's principle of differentiation to Jakobson's principle of binary polarization; from Althusser's special notion of scientific progress to Foucault's total denial of scientific progress; from the early inversion of base and super-structure by Saussure and Lévi-Strauss and Lacan to the more thoroughgoing inversion of base and superstructure by Derrida and Deleuze and Guattari and Baudrillard – the story of Superstructuralism is a story of self-purification and intensification.

Superstructuralism thus unfolds logically as well as chronolo-gically. When its initial approach generates contradictions, it resolves them by moving on to a deeper theoretical level; and when this level in turn generates contradictions, it moves on to deeper levels again. In this respect, Superstructuralism not only bears a general resemblance to Metaphysical philosophy, but actually recapitulates the Hegelian dialectic in its own trajectory.

However, this is not to say that Superstructuralism 'im-proves' all the way from the earliest Structuralists to the latest Post-Structuralists. It is true that Deleuze and Guattari and Baudrillard (for instance) have removed themselves beyond the reach of many attacks to which the earlier Structuralists were vulnerable. But the price of such invulnerability is a kind of philosophical extremism beyond the reach of all ordinary intel-ligibility. When Deleuze and Guattari proclaim the virtues of schizophrenia, or when Baudrillard embraces the prospect of annihilation for its own sake, then we may well feel that the relative inconsistencies of the earlier Structuralists were preferable.

The trouble is that Superstructuralism unfolds in the direc-tion of absolute philosophical truth (or, in Post-Structuralist terms, perpetual philosophical viability). Such is the goal towards which the vertical process of theoretical deepening and auto-critique and self-purification quite properly leads. But this goal has always been, and continues to be, elusive. No philosophy has ever produced lasting or generally acceptable conclusions. Lockean Empiricism, Kantian Transcendental-ism, Husserlian Phenomenology, Logical Positivism – all such movements invariably seem to run themselves into ultimately untenable and embarrassing positions. And Superstructuralism, I suggest, is no exception. The story of Superstructuralism is not the kind of story which lends itself to a happy-ever-after kind of ending. It is the kind of story which peters out.

But on the way – on the way, there are a host of relative truths to be garnered. Throughout its development, and on the various different levels involved in its development, Superstructuralism throws off insights and illuminations. Such is the virtue of any new philosophical perspective which challenges the obvious taken-for-granted face of things; and Superstructuralism possesses this virtue to a particularly high degree. In the last analysis, it is not the goal of the voyage that counts, but the discoveries along the way.

Appendix:
A Superstructuralist
chronology

(Unless otherwise specified, all dates are dates of first publication.)

1900	Freud: *Die Traumdeutung*
1901–2	Durkheim and Mauss: 'De quelques formes primitives de classification'
1907–11	Saussure delivers his Course in General Linguistics
1912	Durkheim: *Les Formes élémentaires de la vie religieuse*
1925	Mauss: *Essai sur le don*
1933–9	Kojève lectures at l'Ecole Pratique des Hautes Etudes
1936	Lacan presents a paper on 'La Stade du miroir' to the International Psychoanalytic Association
1939	Benveniste: 'Nature du signe linguistique'
	Jakobson: 'Zur Structur des Phonems'
1941	Lévi-Strauss and Jakobson meet at the New York School of Social Research
1943	Hjelmslev: *Omkring Sprogteoriens Grundloeggelse*
1949	Lévi-Strauss: *Les Structures élémentaires de la parenté*
1953	Paris Psychoanalytic Association splits
	Lacan delivers the 'Discours de Rome'
1956	Lacan begins his Seminars

1957	Barthes: *Mythologies*
1960	Founding of *Tel Quel*
1961	Foucault: *Folie et déraison: histoire de la folie à l'âge classique*
1963	Lévi-Strauss: *Le Totemisme aujourd'hui* and *La Pensée sauvage*
1964	Barthes: *Eléments de sémiologie*
	Lévi-Strauss: *Le Cru et le cuit*
1965	Althusser: *Pour Marx* and *Lire le Capital* (original edition)
1966	Foucault: *Les Mots et les choses*
	Greimas: *Sémantique structurale*
1967	Barthes: *Système de la mode*
	Derrida: *L'Ecriture et la différence, De la grammatologie, La Voix et la phénomène*
1968	Student revolution in Paris (May)
1969	Foucault: *L'Archéologie du savoir*
	Kristeva: Σημειωτιχὴ
1972	Baudrillard: *Pour une critique de l'économie politique du signe*
	Deleuze and Guattari: *L'Anti-Oedipe*
	Derrida: *La Dissémination, Positions, Marges de la philosophie*
1973	Baudrillard: *Le Miroir de la production*
1975	Foucault: *Surveiller et punir*
1976	Foucault: *Histoire de la sexualité: Vol. 1*

Notes

Introduction
1 I shall touch further upon the relation between Superstructuralism and the Symbolist poets in Chapter 11, section (ii); and I shall demonstrate an important relation between Superstructuralism and Marcel Proust in Chapter 5, section (iii).

1 Saussure and the concept of 'langue'
1 Ferdinand de Saussure, 1959, *Course in General Linguistics*, ed. Charles Bally and Albert Sechehaye, in collaboration with Albert Reidlinger, trans. Wade Baskin (New York: The Philosophical Library), 14.
2 ibid., 119.
3 ibid., 118.
4 ibid., 117.
5 ibid., 87.
6 V. 'Knowledge by acquaintance and knowledge by description', in Bertrand Russell, 1918, *Mysticism and Logic, and Other Essays*, (London: Longmans, Green & Co.); and 'The philosophy of logical atomism', in Bertrand Russell, 1956, *Logic and Knowledge: Essays 1901–1950*, ed. R.C. Marsh (London: Allen & Unwin).
7 V. 'On denoting', in *Logic and Knowledge: Essays 1901–1950*.
8 V. Claude Lévi-Strauss, 1966, *The Savage Mind* (London: Weidenfeld & Nicolson), 197 et seq.; Umberto Eco, 1976, *A Theory of Semiotics* (Bloomington: Indiana University Press), 86–8; and Jacques Derrida, 1976, *Of Grammatology*, trans. Gayatri Chakravorty Spivak (Baltimore: Johns Hopkins University Press), 89.
9 For more on this, V. Chapter 6, section (i).

10 For more on this, v. Chapter 10, section (ii), and Chapter 11, section (ii).

2   From Durkheim to Lévi-Strauss

1 Emile Durkheim, 1947, *Division of Labour in Society*, trans. George Simpson (Glencoe, Ill.: The Free Press), 338–9.
2 Emile Durkheim, 1953, *Sociology and Philosophy*, trans. D. F. Pocock (Glencoe, Ill.: The Free Press), 25.
3 Emile Durkheim, 1976, *The Elementary Forms of the Religious Life*, trans. J. W. Swain (London: Allen & Unwin), 40.
4 ibid., 206.
5 ibid., 41.
6 V. Durkheim's review of Kohler, 1898, *Zur Urgeschichte der Ehe*, in *Année sociologique*, I, 306–9; v. Mauss, 1920, in 'L'Extension du potlatch en Mélanésie', in *Anthropologie*, xxx, 396–7.
7 Claude Lévi-Strauss, 1949, *Les Structures elémentaires de la parenté* (Paris: Presses Universitaires de France), 595.
8 V. especially, 1972, 'Structural analysis in linguistics and in anthropology', in *Structural Anthropology*, trans. Claire Jacobson and B. Grundfest Schoepf (Harmondsworth: Penguin), 31–54.
9 Claude Lévi-Strauss, 1966, *The Savage Mind* (London: Weidenfeld & Nicolson), 75.
10 ibid., 268.
11 ibid., 107.
12 ibid., 144.
13 Claude Lévi-Strauss, 1973, *From Honey to Ashes: Introduction to a Science of Mythology*, Vol. 2, trans. John and Doreen Weightman (London: Jonathan Cape), 467.
14 *The Savage Mind*, 223.

3   Lacan's Freud

1 Jacques Lacan, 1979, *The Four Fundamental Concepts of Psychoanalysis*, trans. Alan Sheridan (Harmondsworth: Penguin), 20.
2 Jacques Lacan, 1972, 'The insistence of the letter in the unconscious', in *The Structuralists: From Marx to Lévi-Strauss*, ed. Richel and Fernando de George (New York: Doubleday Anchor), 316.
3 Jacques Lacan, 1968, *The Language of the Self*, trans. Anthony Wilden (New York: Delta Books), 27.
4 ibid., 16.
5 Jacques Lacan, 1977, *Écrits: A Selection*, trans. Alan Sheridan (London: Tavistock), 284.
6 ibid., 23.
7 ibid., 13.
8 ibid., 4.

9 ibid., 137.
10 ibid., 286.

4 Althusser's Marx

1 Louis Althusser, 1971, *Lenin and Philosophy and Other Essays*, trans. Ben Brewster (New York: Monthly Review Press), 218.

2 Louis Althusser, 1972, *Politics and History: Montesquieu, Rousseau, Hegel and Marx*, trans. Ben Brewster (London: New Left Books), 25.

3 *Lenin and Philosophy and Other Essays*, 182.

4 Quoted in *Politics and History*, 150, from Rousseau, 1966, *The Social Contract and Other Discourses*, trans. G. D. H. Cole (London: Dent) 23.

5 Louis Althusser, 1976, *Essays in Self-Criticism*, trans. Grahame Locke (London: New Left Books), 198.

6 Louis Althusser, 1969, *For Marx*, trans. Ben Brewster (London: New Left Books), 233.

7 ibid.

8 *Lenin and Philosophy and Other Essays*, 171.

9 ibid., 181.

10 *For Marx*, 235.

11 ibid.

12 V. the opening pages of 'Ideology and ideological state apparatuses', in *Lenin and Philosophy and Other Essays*.

13 V. *For Marx*, 114–16.

14 *Lenin and Philosophy and Other Essays*, 147.

5 Barthes and Semiotics

1 V. 'Steak and chips', in Roland Barthes, 1973, *Mythologies*, trans. Annette Lavers (St Albans: Paladin), 62–4.

2 ibid., 62.

3 V. 'Wine and milk', in *Mythologies*, 58–61.

4 ibid., 58.

5 ibid., 59.

6 V. 'Rhetoric of the image', in Roland Barthes, 1977, *Image-Music-Text*, trans. Stephen Heath (Glasgow: Fontana/Collins), 32–51.

7 V. *Mythologies*, 124–5.

8 *Image-Music-Text*, 38.

9 V. *Mythologies*, 41–2.

10 V. 'Soap powders and detergents', in *Mythologies*, 36–8.

11 Robert Musil, 1968, *The Man Without Qualities*, Vol. 1, trans. Eithne Wilkins and Ernst Kaiser (London: Panther Books), 376.

12 Roland Barthes, 1968, *Elements of Semiology*, trans. Annette Lavers and Colin Smith (New York: Hill & Wang), 46.

Part Two   Preliminaries

1 V. Louis Althusser, 1971, *Lenin and Philosophy and Other Essays*, trans. Ben Brewster (New York: Monthly Review Press), 205.

6 Metaphysical philosophy

1 F. H. Bradley, 1962, *Ethical Studies* (Oxford: Oxford University Press), 171–2.

2 V. especially the chapter on 'Marx's immense theoretical revolution' in Louis Althusser and Etienne Balibar, 1970, *Reading Capital*, trans. Ben Brewster (London: New Left Books), 182–93.

7 More Structural Linguistics

1 Ferdinand de Saussure, 1959, *Course in General Linguistics*, ed. Charles Bally and Albert Sechehaye, in collaboration with Albert Reidlinger, trans. Wade Baskin (New York: The Philosophical Library), 15.

2 ibid., 113.

3 Emile Benveniste, 1971, *Problems in General Linguistics*, trans. Mary Elizabeth Meek (Coral Gables: University of Miami Press), 45.

4 *Course in General Linguistics*, 117, 113.

5 *Problems in General Linguistics*, 47.

6 ibid., 46.

7 *Course in General Linguistics*, 116.

8 ibid., 123.

9 ibid., 23, quoted in Roman Jakobson and Morris Halle, 1956, *Fundamentals of Language* (s'-Gravenhage: Mouton), 61. V. also Roman Jakobson, 1962, *Selected Writings*, I (s'-Gravenhage: Mouton), 419–20, 636 and 653.

10 V. *Selected Writings*, I, 231, 420, 636.

11 ibid., 421.

12 ibid., 303, this passage trans. from the German by Jan Bruck.

13 V. 'Two aspects of language and two types of aphasic disturbances', in *Fundamentals of Language*, 55–82.

14 *Fundamentals of Language*, 37.

15 ibid., 47.

16 Louis Hjelmslev, 1961, *Prolegomena to a Theory of Language*, trans. Francis J. Whitfield, revised English edition (Wisconsin: University of Wisconsin Press).

17 A. J. Greimas, 1966, *Sémantique structurale: recherche de méthode* (Paris: Larousse), 36, my trans.

18 ibid., 33, my trans.

8 Althusser and science

1 For Althusser's confession of his relation to Spinoza, v. 1969, *Essays*

in Self-Criticism, trans. Grahame Locke (London: New Left Books), 132.

2 Karl Marx, 1970, *A Contribution to the Critique of Political Economy*, trans. S. W. Ryazanskaya (Moscow: Progress Publishers), 205.

3 Louis Althusser, 1969, *For Marx*, trans. Ben Brewster (London: New Left Books), 183–4.

4 Louis Althusser and Etienne Balibar, 1970, *Reading Capital*, trans. Ben Brewster (London: New Left Books), 141.

5 ibid., 42.

6 ibid., 59.

7 *For Marx*, 184–5.

8 ibid., 170, 168.

9 *Reading Capital*, 159.

10 ibid., 158.

11 ibid.

12 ibid., 150–3.

13 ibid., 40.

14 ibid., 190.

15 V. Ted Benton, 1977, *Philosophical Foundations of the Three Sociologies* (London: Routledge & Kegan Paul); Terry Lovell, 1980, *Pictures of Reality: Aesthetics, Politics, Pleasure* (London: British Film Institute); Barry Hindess and Paul Hirst, 1977, *Mode of Production and Social Formations* (London: Macmillan).

16 *A Contribution to the Critique of Political Economy*, 206.

17 V. *Essays in Self-Criticism*, 129, 140.

18 Louis Althusser, 1971, *Lenin and Philosophy and Other Essays*, trans. Ben Brewster (New York: Monthly Review Press), 113–4.

19 ibid., 115.

20 *For Marx*, 186.

9 Foucault as archaeologist

1 Michel Foucault, 1973, *The Birth of the Clinic: An Archaeology of Medical Perception*, trans. A. M. Sheridan Smith (London: Tavistock), 195.

2 ibid., 196.

3 ibid., 195.

4 Michel Foucault, 1973, *Madness and Civilization: A History of Insanity in the Age of Reason*, trans. Richard Howard (New York: Vintage Books), 271.

5 ibid., 276.

6 Michel Foucault, 1972, *The Archaeology of Knowledge*, trans. A. M. Sheridan Smith (London: Tavistock), 146.

7 V. Alexander Kojève, 1969, *Introduction to the Reading of Hegel*, trans. James H. Nicholls, Jnr, ed. Allan Bloom (New York: Basic Books).

8 Emile Durkheim, 1976, *The Elementary Forms of the Religious Life*, trans. Joseph Ward Swain (London: Allen & Unwin), 439.
9 ibid.
10 ibid., 17.
11 Michel Foucault, 1970, *The Order of Things* (London: Tavistock), 296.
12 ibid., 132.
13 ibid., 120.
14 ibid., 251.
15 ibid., 268.
16 ibid., 297.
17 ibid., 313.
18 ibid., 363–4.
19 ibid., 379.
20 *The Archaeology of Knowledge*, 8.
21 *The Order of Things*, 374.
22 ibid., 375, 376.
23 ibid., 315.
24 ibid., 338.
25 ibid., 305, 306.
26 ibid., 305.
27 *The Archaeology of Knowledge*, 205.
28 ibid.

10 Derrida and language as Writing

1 Jacques Derrida, 1973, *Speech and Phenomena, and Other Essays on Husserl's Theory of Signs*, trans. David B. Allison (Evanston: Northwestern University Press), 33.
2 ibid., 76.
3 ibid., 92.
4 Jacques Derrida, 1982, *Margins of Philosophy*, trans. Alan Bass (Chicago: University of Chicago Press), 316.
5 ibid.
6 Jacques Derrida, 1976, *Of Grammatology*, trans. Gayatri Chakravorty Spivak (Baltimore: Johns Hopkins University Press), 37.
7 For Derrida's counter-attack upon Husserl's attitude to mathematics, v. Jacques Derrida, 1978, *Edmund Husserl's Origin of Geometry: An Introduction*, trans. John P. Leavey, Jnr (Stony Brook: Nicholas Hays).
8 *Speech and Phenomena*, 89.
9 *Of Grammatology*, 136.
10 Jacques Derrida, 1978, *Writing and Difference*, trans. Alan Bass (London: Routledge & Kegan Paul), 178.
11 V. *Of Grammatology*, Part II, Chapters 2–4.
12 *Writing and Difference*, 212.

13 Jacques Derrida, 1981, *Dissemination*, trans. Barbara Johnson (London: The Athlone Press), 95.
14 V. ibid., 129, 140, 142.
15 V. *Writing and Difference*, 27, 29.
16 *Dissemination*, 129–30.
17 *Writing and Difference*, 25.
18 *Dissemination*, 149.
19 ibid., 6.
20 *Speech and Phenomena*, in 'Différance', 141.
21 Jacques Derrida, 1981, *Positions*, trans. Alan Bass (Chicago: University of Chicago Press), 27.
22 *Writing and Difference*, 5.
23 ibid., 4.
24 *Speech and Phenomena*, in 'Différance', 129.
25 *Positions*, 9.
26 *Speech and Phenomena*, in 'Différance', 148.
27 Footnote by Koyré, quoted by Derrida in *Speech and Phenonema*, in 'Differance', 144.
28 *Positions*, 43.
29 V. the essay 'From restricted to general economy', in *Writing and Difference*.

11 Derrida's general theory of Writing

1 Jacques Derrida, 1981, *Positions*, trans. Alan Bass (Chicago: University of Chicago Press), 41.
2 V. Jacques Derrida, 1978, *Writing and Difference*, trans. Alan Bass (London: Routledge & Kegan Paul), 226.
3 ibid., 224.
4 Jacques Derrida, 1976, *Of Grammatology*, trans. Gayatri Chakravorty Spivak (Baltimore: Johns Hopkins University Press), 49.
5 *Writing and Difference*, 224.
6 Jacques Derrida, 1973, *Speech and Phenomena, and Other Essays on Husserl's Theory of Signs*, trans. D.B. Allison (Evanston, Ill.: Northwestern University Press), in 'Différance', 152.
7 *Writing and Difference*, 219.
8 ibid., 218.
9 V. *Positions*, 82.
10 ibid., 64.
11 *Of Grammatology*, 47.
12 ibid., 49–50.
13 *Positions*, 64.
14 *Writing and Difference*, 215, as quoted from Freud, 1958, *Standard Edition of the Complete Psychological Works of Sigmund Freud*, Vol. V, ed. James Strachey, (London: Hogarth Press), 611.
15 ibid., 201.

16 *Speech and Phenomena*, in 'Différance', 150.
17 ibid., 158.
18 *Writing and Difference*, 11.
19 ibid., 211, 213.
20 *Of Grammatology*, 107–8.
21 *Writing and Difference*, 259.
22 ibid., 8.
23 *Of Grammatology*, 87.
24 V. especially the essay *Ur-Geräusch*, in Rilke, 1966, *Werke in Drei Bänden*, III (Frankfurt-am-Main: Insel Verlag), 543–50.
25 V. 'From restricted to general economy: a Hegelianism without reserve', in *Writing and Difference*, especially 254–62.

12 Foucault as genealogist

1 Michel Foucault, 1980, *Power/Knowledge*, ed. Colin Gordon (Brighton: Harvester Press), 83, 117.
2 For Foucault's animosity towards Derrida, v. especially, 1972, 'Mon corps, ce papier, ce feu', published as an appendix to the second French edition of *Folie et déraison*, 1972 (Paris: Gallimard).
3 *Power/Knowledge*, 114.
4 ibid., 197.
5 Michel Foucault, 1979, *Michel Foucault: Power, Truth, Strategy*, ed. Meaghan Morris and Paul Patton (Sydney: Feral Publications), 69–70.
6 Michel Foucault, 1977, *Discipline and Punish*, trans. Alan Sheridan (London: Allen Lane), 25.
7 *Power/Knowledge*, 119.
8 ibid., 125.
9 Michel Foucault, 1980, *The History of Sexuality, Volume 1: An Introduction*, trans. Robert Hurley (New York: Vintage Books), 4–5.
10 ibid., 60.
11 Michel Foucault, 1977, *Language, Counter-Memory, Practice*, ed. Donald Bouchard (Oxford: Basil Blackwell), 153.
12 *Power/Knowledge*, 56–7.
13 *The History of Sexuality*, 23.
14 ibid., 152.
15 ibid., 115.
16 ibid., 137.
17 ibid., 42.
18 ibid., 155.
19 ibid., 71, 57.
20 ibid., 157.
21 *Power/Knowledge*, 39.
22 *The History of Sexuality*, 95.

23 *Power/Knowledge*, 31.
24 ibid.
25 *Discipline and Punish*, 274.
26 ibid., 183.
27 ibid., 277.
28 ibid., 26.
29 *Power/Knowledge*, 190.
30 *Michel Foucault: Power, Truth, Strategy*, 62. Quoted from notes on a lecture given by Foucault at the Collège de France, 28 March 1973.
31 ibid.

13 More Post-Structuralists

1 Julia Kristeva, 1975, 'The system and the speaking subject', in *The Tell-Tale Sign*, ed. Thomas Sebeok (Lisse: The Peter de Ridder Press), 48.
2 Roland Barthes, interview in 'Réponses', Autumn 1971, *Tel Quel*, 47, p. 97.
3 Julia Kristeva, 1980, *Desire in Language*, ed. Leon S. Roudiez (Oxford: Basil Blackwell), 111.
4 Julia Kristeva, 1974, *La Révolution du langage poétique* (Paris: Seuil), 188, my trans.
5 Kristeva, *Desire in Language*, 36; Barthes, *Image-Music-Text*, 157.
6 Julia Kristeva, 1969, Σημειωτιχὴ: *Recherches pour une sémanalyse* (Paris: Seuil), 279, my trans.
7 V. *Image-Music-Text*, 147.
8 *Desire in Language*, 36.
9 ibid., 65.
10 Roland Barthes, 1976, *The Pleasure of the Text*, trans. Richard Miller (London: Jonathan Cape), 17.
11 'The system and the speaking subject', in *The Tell-Tale Sign*, 51.
12 ibid.
13 ibid., 50.
14 Gillès Deleuze and Félix Guattari, 1977, *Anti-Oedipus*, trans. Robert Hurley, Mark Seem and Helen R. Lane (New York: Viking Press), 120, 275.
15 ibid., 30.
16 ibid., 46.
17 ibid., 97, 98.
18 ibid., 88.
19 ibid., 86.
20 ibid., 23.
21 ibid., 12.
22 ibid., 76.
23 ibid., 328.

24 Gillès Deleuze, 1980, 'The schizophrenic and language: surface and depth in Lewis Carroll and Antonin Artaud', in *Textual Strategies: Perspectives in Post-Structuralist Criticism*, ed. Josué V. Harrari (London: Methuen), 287, 291.

25 *Anti-Oedipus*, 55.

26 ibid., 53.

27 ibid., 40.

28 ibid., 31.

29 ibid., 361.

30 ibid., 347.

31 ibid., 33.

32 ibid., 257.

33 ibid., 239–40.

34 V. Jean Baudrillard, 1982, 'Oublier Foucault', in *Local Consumption* (Sydney: Theoretical Strategies Issue); and Jean Baudrillard, 1975, *The Mirror of Production*, trans. Mark Poster (St Louis: Telos Press), 17–18.

35 Jean Baudrillard, 1981, *For a Critique of the Political Economy of the Sign*, trans. Charles Levin (St Louis: Telos Press), 155.

36 ibid., 63.

37 ibid., 80–1.

38 *The Mirror of Production*, 79.

39 ibid., 31.

40 ibid., 156.

41 *For a Critique of the Political Economy of the Sign*, 153.

42 *The Mirror of Production*, 121.

43 *For a Critique of the Political Economy of the Sign*, 92.

44 *The Mirror of Production*, 121.

45 ibid.

46 ibid., 122.

47 *For a Critique of the Political Economy of the Sign*, 98.

48 ibid.

49 ibid., 97.

50 ibid.

51 ibid., 135.

52 *The Mirror of Production*, 82.

53 *For a Critique of the Political Economy of the Sign*, 132.

54 V. Claude Lévi-Strauss, 1976, *Tristes Tropiques*, trans. John and Doreen Weightman (Harmondsworth: Penguin), 398.

55 *For a Critique of the Political Economy of the Sign*, 64.

56 Jean Baudrillard, 1983, *In the Shadow of the Silent Majorities*, trans. Paul Foss, Paul Patton and John Johnston (New York: Semiotext(e)), 46.

Bibliography

1(A)   Primary material

Althusser, Louis, 1969, *For Marx*, trans. Ben Brewster (London: New Left Books).

—— 1971, *Lenin and Philosophy and Other Essays*, trans. Ben Brewster (New York: Monthly Review Press).

—— 1972, *Politics and History: Montesquieu, Rousseau, Hegel and Marx*, trans. Ben Brewster (London: New Left Books).

—— 1976, *Essays in Self-Criticism*, trans. Grahame Lock (London: New Left Books).

Althusser, Louis and Balibar, Etienne, 1970, *Reading Capital*, trans. Ben Brewster (London: New Left Books).

Barthes, Roland, 1968, *Elements of Semiology*, trans. Annette Lavers and Colin Smith (New York: Hill & Wang).

—— 1972, *Critical Essays*, trans. Richard Howard (Evanston: North-western University Press).

—— 1973, *Mythologies*, trans. Annette Lavers (St Albans: Paladin).

—— 1975, *S/Z*, trans. Richard Miller (London: Jonathan Cape).

—— 1976, *The Pleasure of the Text*, trans. Richard Miller (London: Jonathan Cape).

—— 1977, *Image-Music-Text*, trans. Stephen Heath (Glasgow: Fontana/Collins).

—— 1977, *Roland Barthes by Roland Barthes*, trans. Richard Howard (London: Macmillan).

—— 1979, *The Eiffel Tower*, trans. Richard Howard (New York: Hill & Wang).

—— 1982, *A Barthes Reader*, ed. Susan Sontag (London: Jonathan Cape).

—— 1983, *The Fashion System*, trans. Matthew Ward and Richard Howard (New York: Hill & Wang).

—— 1984, *Camera Lucida*, trans. Richard Howard (London: Fontana).

—— 1985, *The Grain of the Voice: Interviews 1962–80*, trans. Linda Coverdale (New York: Hill & Wang).

Baudrillard, Jean, 1975, *The Mirror of Production*, trans. Mark Poster (St Louis: Telos Press).

—— 1981, *For a Critique of the Political Economy of the Sign*, trans. Charles Levin (St Louis: Telos Press).

—— 1983, *In the Shadow of the Silent Majorities . . . Or, The End of the Social and Other Essays*, trans. Paul Foss, Paul Patton and John Johnston (New York: Semiotext(e)).

—— 1983, *Simulations*, trans. Paul Foss, Paul Patton and Philip Beitchman (New York: Semiotext(e)).

Benveniste, Emile, 1971, *Problems in General Linguistics*, trans. Mary Elizabeth Meek (Coral Gables: University of Miami Press).

Deleuze, Gillès and Guattari, Félix, 1977, *Anti-Oedipus: Capitalism and Schizophrenia*, trans. Robert Hurley, Mark Seem and Helen R. Lane (New York: Viking Press).

—— Spring 1981, 'Rhizome', trans. Paul Foss and Paul Patton, *I & C*, VIII, pp. 49–72.

Derrida, Jacques, 1973, *Speech and Phenomena, and Other Essays on Husserl's Theory of Signs*, trans. David B. Allison (Evanston: Northwestern University Press).

—— 1976, *Of Grammatology*, trans. Gayatri Chakravorty Spivak (Baltimore: Johns Hopkins University Press).

—— 1978, *Edmund Husserl's Origin of Geometry: An Introduction*, trans. John P. Leavey, Jnr (Stony Brook: Nicholas Hays).

—— 1978, *Writing and Difference*, trans. Alan Bass (Chicago: University of Chicago Press).

—— 1979, *Spurs: Nietzsche's Styles*, trans. Barbara Harlow (Chicago: University of Chicago Press).

—— 1981, *Dissemination*, trans. Barbara Johnson (London: Athlone Press).

—— 1981, *Positions*, trans. Alan Bass (Chicago: University of Chicago Press).

—— 1982, *Margins of Philosophy*, trans. Alan Bass (Chicago: University of Chicago Press).

Durkheim, Emile, 1976, *The Elementary Forms of the Religious Life*, trans. Joseph Ward Swain (London: Allen & Unwin).

Durkheim, Emile and Mauss, Marcel, 1963, *Primitive Classification*, trans. Rodney Needham (Chicago: University of Chicago Press).

Eco, Umberto, 1976, *A Theory of Semiotics* (Bloomington: Indiana University Press).

Foucault, Michel, 1970, *The Order of Things* (London: Tavistock).

—— 1972, *The Archaeology of Knowledge*, trans. A. M. Sheridan Smith (London: Tavistock).

—— 1972, 'The Discourse on Language', published as an appendix to *The Archaeology of Knowledge*, trans. A. M. Sheridan Smith (New York: Pantheon).

—— 1973, *The Birth of the Clinic: An Archaeology of Medical Perception*, trans. A. M. Sheridan Smith (London: Tavistock).

—— 1973, *Madness and Civilization: A History of Insanity in the Age of Reason*, trans. Richard Howard (New York: Vintage Books).

—— 1977, *Discipline and Punish*, trans. Alan Sheridan (London: Allen Lane).

—— 1977, *Language, Counter-Memory, Practice*, ed. Donald F. Bouchard (Oxford: Basil Blackwell).

—— Spring 1978, 'Politics and the Study of Discourse', *I & C*, III, pp. 7–26.

—— Autumn 1979, 'On Governmentality', *I & C*, VI, pp. 5–22.

—— 1980, *The History of Sexuality, Vol. I: An Introduction*, trans. Robert Hurley (New York: Vintage Books).

—— 1980, *Power/Knowledge*, ed. Colin Gordon (Brighton: Harvester Press).

—— Spring 1981, 'Questions of Method: An Interview with Michel Foucault', *I & C*, VIII, pp. 3–14.

Greimas, A. J., 1966, *Sémantique structurale* (Paris: Larousse).

Guiraud, Pierre, 1975, *Semiology*, trans. George Gross (London: Routledge & Kegan Paul).

Hjelmslev, Louis, 1961, *Prologomena to a Theory of Language*, trans. Francis J. Whitfield (Wisconsin: University of Wisconsin Press).

Jakobson, Roman, 1962 and 1971, *Selected Writings, Vol. 1 (Phonological Studies) and Vol. 2 (Word and Language)* (s'-Gravenhage: Mouton).

Jakobson, Roman, and Halle, Morris, 1956, *Fundamentals of Language* (s'-Gravenhage: Mouton).

Kojève, Alexandre, 1969, *Introduction to the Reading of Hegel*, trans. James H. Nicholls, Jnr (New York: Basic Books).

Kristeva, Julia, 1969, Σημειωτιχὴ: *Recherches pour une sémanalyse* (Paris: Seuil).

—— 1974, *La Révolution du langage poétique* (Paris: Seuil).

—— 1980, *Desire in Language*, ed. Leon S. Roudiez (Oxford: Basil Blackwell).

Lacan, Jacques, 1968, *The Language of the Self*, trans. Anthony Wilden (New York: Delta Books).

—— 1977, *Ecrits: A Selection*, trans. Alan Sheridan (London: Tavistock).

—— 1979, *The Four Fundamental Concepts of Psychoanalysis*, trans. Alan Sheridan (Harmondsworth: Penguin).

Lévi-Strauss, Claude, 1949, *Les Structures élémentaires de la parenté* (Paris: P.U.F.).

—— 1966, *The Savage Mind* (London: Weidenfeld & Nicolson).

—— 1969, *Totemism*, trans. Rodney Needham (Harmondsworth: Penguin).

—— 1970, *The Raw and the Cooked: Introduction to a Science of Mythology: 1*, trans. John and Doreen Weightman (London: Jonathan Cape).

—— 1972, *Structural Anthropology*, trans. Claire Jacobson and Brooke Grundfest Schoepf (Harmondsworth: Penguin).

—— 1973, *From Honey to Ashes: Introduction to a Science of Mythology: 2*, trans. John and Doreen Weightman (London: Jonathan Cape).

—— 1976, *Tristes Tropiques*, trans. John and Doreen Weightman (Harmondsworth: Penguin).

—— 1978, *Myth and Meaning* (London: Routledge & Kegan Paul).

—— 1978, *The Origin of Table Manners: Introduction to a Science of Mythology: 3*, trans. John and Doreen Weightman (London: Jonathan Cape).

—— 1978, *Structural Anthropology 2*, trans. Monique Layton (Harmondsworth: Penguin).

—— 1981, *The Naked Man: Introduction to a Science of Mythology: 4*, trans. John and Doreen Weightman (London: Jonathan Cape).

Mauss, Marcel, 1967, *The Gift*, trans. Ian Cunison (New York: Norton).

Saussure, Ferdinand de, 1959, *Course in General Linguistics*, ed. Charles Bally and Albert Sechehaye in collaboration with Albert Reidlinger, trans. Wade Baskin (New York: The Philosophical Library).

1(B) Collections containing primary material

De George, Richard and De George, Fernande (eds), 1972, *The Structuralists: From Marx to Lévi-Strauss* (New York: Doubleday Anchor).

Ehrmann, Jacques (ed.), 1970, *Structuralism* (New York: Doubleday Anchor).

Harrari, Josué V. (ed.), 1980, *Textual Strategies: Perspectives in Post-Structuralist Criticism* (London: Methuen).

Lane, Michael (ed.), 1970, *Introduction to Structuralism* (New York: Basic Books).

Macksey, Richard and Donato, Eugenio (eds), 1970, *The Structuralist Controversy: The Languages of Criticism and the Sciences of Man* (Baltimore: Johns Hopkins University Press).

Morris, Meaghan and Patton, Paul (eds), 1979, *Michel Foucault: Power, Truth, Strategy* (Sydney: Feral Publications).

Schneiderman, Stuart (ed.), 1980, *Returning to Freud: Clinical Psychoanalysis in the School of Lacan* (New Haven: Yale University Press).

Sebéok, Thomas (ed.), 1975, *The Tell-Tale Sign* (Lisse: The Peter de Ridder Press).

Young, Robert (ed.), 1981, *Untying the Text: A Post-Structuralist Reader* (London: Routledge & Kegan Paul).

2 Secondary material

Badcock, C. R., 1976, *Lévi-Strauss: Structuralism and Sociological Theory* (New York: Holmes & Meier).

Bailey, R. W., Matjeka, L. and Steiner, P. (eds), 1978, *The Sign: Semiotics Around the World* (Ann Arbor: Michigan Publications).

Benoist, Jean-Marie, 1978, *The Structural Revolution* (London: Weidenfeld & Nicolson).

Boon, James A., 1972, *From Symbolism to Structuralism: Lévi-Strauss in a Literary Tradition* (Oxford: Basil Blackwell).

Broekman, Jan M., 1974, *Structuralism: Moscow, Prague, Paris*, trans. Jan F. Beekman and Brunhilde Helm (Dordrecht: D. Reidl).

Callinicos, Alex, 1976, *Althusser's Marxism* (London: Pluto Press).

Clarke, Simon, 1981, *The Foundations of Structuralism: A Critique of Lévi-Strauss and the Structuralist Movement* (Brighton: Harvester Press).

Clarke, Simon, Lovell, Terry, McDonnell, Kevin, Robins, Kevin and Seidler, Victor, 1980, *One-Dimensional Marxism: Althusser and the Politics of Culture* (London: Allison & Busby).

Clément, Catherine, 1983, *The Lives and Legends of Jacques Lacan*, trans. Arthur Goldhammer (New York: Columbia University Press).

Cousins, Mark and Hussain, Athar, 1984, *Michel Foucault* (London: Macmillan).

Coward, Rosalind and Ellis, John, 1977, *Language and Materialism: Developments in Semiology and the Theory of the Subject* (London: Routledge & Kegan Paul).

Culler, Jonathan, 1973, *Structuralist Poetics: Structuralism, Linguistics and the Study of Literature* (London: Routledge & Kegan Paul).

—— 1981, *The Pursuit of Signs: Semiotics, Literature, Deconstruction* (London: Routledge & Kegan Paul).

—— 1982, *On Deconstruction: Theory and Criticism after Structuralism* (Ithaca, NY: Cornell University Press).

—— 1983, *Barthes* (Glasgow: Fontana/Collins).

Descombes, Vincent, 1980, *Modern French Philosophy*, trans. L. Scott-Fox and J. M. Harding (Cambridge: Cambridge University Press).

Dreyfus, Hubert L. and Rabinow, Paul, 1982, *Michel Foucault: Beyond Structuralism and Hermeneutics* (Brighton: Harvester Press).

Fekete, John (ed.), 1984, *The Structural Allegory* (Manchester: Manchester University Press).

Frankovits, André (ed.), 1984, *Seduced and Abandoned: The Baudrillard Scene* (Sydney: Stonemoss Services).

Gardner, Howard, 1973, *The Quest for Mind: Piaget, Lévi-Strauss, and the Structuralist Movement* (New York: Knopf).

Glucksmann, Miriam, 1974, *Structuralist Analysis in Contemporary Social Thought* (London: Routledge & Kegan Paul).

Hawkes, Terence, 1977, *Structuralism and Semiotics* (London: Methuen).

Holenstein, Elmar, 1976, *Roman Jakobson's Approach to Language: Phenomenological Structuralism*, trans. Catherine Schelbert and Tarcisius Schelbert (Bloomington: Indiana University Press).

Jameson, Fredric, 1972, *The Prison-House of Language* (Princeton: Princeton University Press).

Korn, Francis, 1973, *Elementary Structures Reconsidered: Lévi-Strauss on Kinship* (London: Tavistock).

Kurzweil, Edith, 1980, *The Age of Structuralism: Lévi-Strauss to Foucault* (New York: Columbia University Press).

Laplanche, Jean and Pontalis, Jean-Baptiste, 1973, *The Language of Psycho-Analysis*, trans. Donald Nicholson-Smith (London: Hogarth Press).

Larrain, Jorge, 1979, *The Concept of Ideology* (London: Hutchinson).

Lavers, Annette, 1982, *Roland Barthes: Structuralism and After* (Cambridge: Harvard University Press).

Leach, Edmund, 1974, *Claude Lévi-Strauss* (New York: Viking Press).

Leitch, Vincent B., 1983, *Deconstructive Criticism* (London: Hutchinson).

Lemaire, Anika, 1977, *Jacques Lacan*, trans. David Macey (London: Routledge & Kegan Paul).

Lemert Charles C. and Gillan, Garth, 1982, *Michel Foucault: Social Theory as Transgression* (New York: Columbia University Press).

Lovell, Terry, 1980, *Pictures of Reality: Aesthetics, Politics, Pleasure* (London: British Film Institute).

MacCannell, Dean and MacCannell, Juliet Flower, 1982, *The Time of the Sign* (Bloomington: Indiana University Press).

Norris, Christopher, 1982, *Deconstruction: Theory and Practice* (London: Methuen).

Pace, David, 1983, *Claude Lévi-Strauss: The Bearer of Ashes* (London: Routledge & Kegan Paul).

Pettit, Phillip, 1975, *The Concept of Structuralism: A Critical Analysis* (Dublin: Gill & Macmillan).

Piaget, Jean, 1970, *Structuralism*, trans. Chaninah Maschler (New York: Basic Books).

Poster, Mark, 1984, *Foucault, Marxism and History* (Cambridge: Polity Press).

Robey, David (ed.), 1973, *Structuralism: An Introduction* (Oxford: Clarendon Press).

Roland, Alan (ed.), 1978, *Psychoanalysis, Creativity and Literature: A French–American Inquiry* (New York: Columbia University Press).

Rossi, Ino (ed.), 1984, *The Unconscious in Culture: The Structuralism of Claude Lévi-Strauss in Perspective* (New York: Dutton).

Schaff, Adam, 1978, *Structuralism and Marxism* (Oxford: Pergamon Press).

Seung, T. K., 1982, *Structuralism and Hermeneutics* (New York: Columbia University Press).

Sheridan, Alan, 1980, *Michel Foucault: The Will to Truth* (London: Tavistock).

Silverman, Kaja, 1983, *The Subject of Semiotics* (New York: Oxford University Press).

Smart, Barry, 1983, *Foucault, Marxism and Critique* (London: Routledge & Kegan Paul).

Stanton, Martin, 1983, *Outside the Dream: Lacan and French Styles of Psychoanalysis* (London: Routledge & Kegan Paul).

Sturrock, John (ed.), 1979, *Structuralism and Since: From Lévi-Strauss to Derrida* (Oxford: Oxford University Press).

Thompson, E. P., 1978, *The Poverty of Theory, and Other Essays* (London: Merlin Press).

Timpanaro, Sebastiano, 1975, *On Materialism*, trans. Laurence Garner (London: New Left Books).

Turkle, Sherry, 1978, *Psychoanalytic Politics: Freud's French Revolution* (New York: Basic Books).

Wilden, Anthony, 1972, *System and Structure: Essays in Communication and Exchange* (London: Tavistock).

Index